Brontë Parsonage MUSEUM

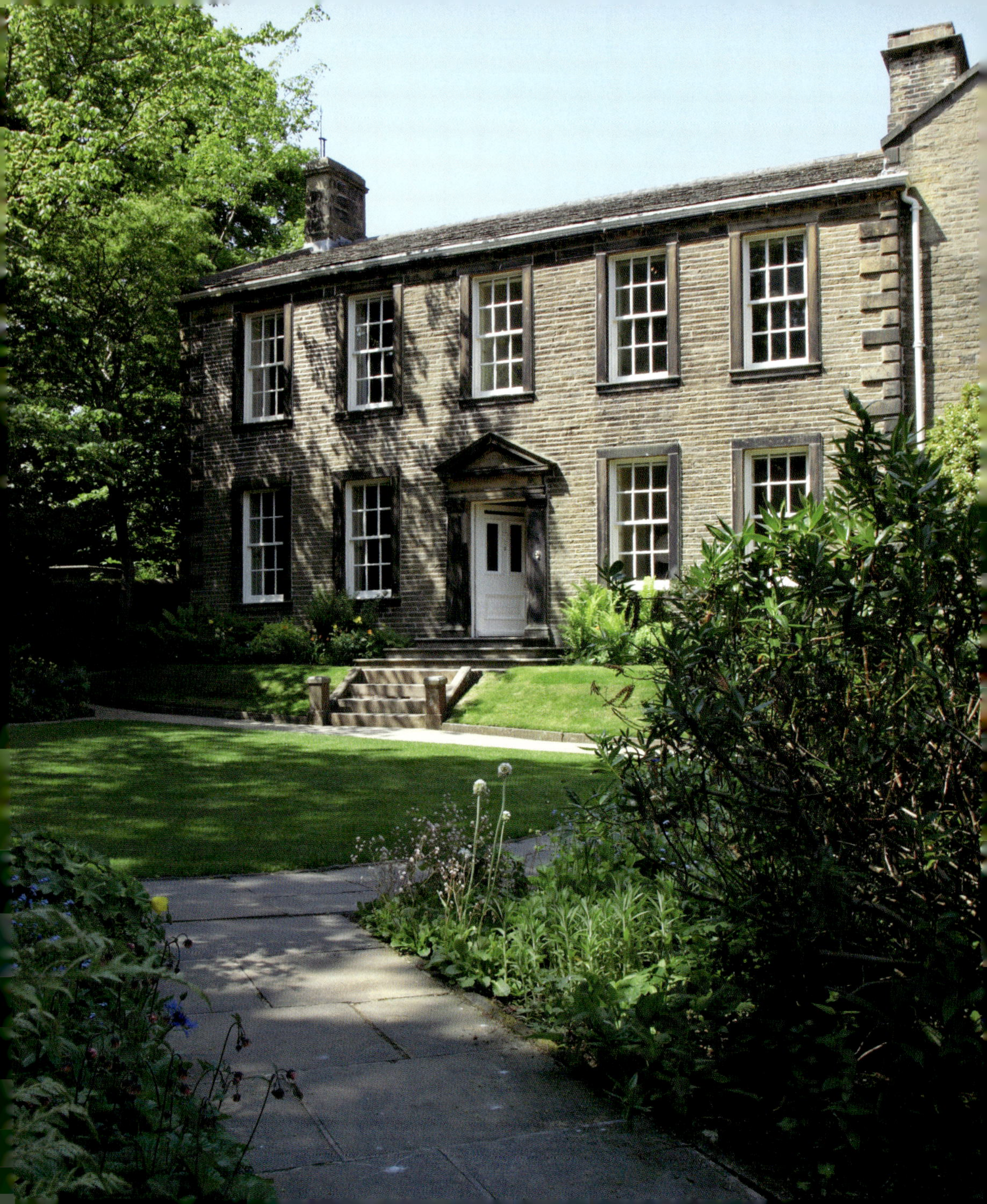

CONTENTS

INTRODUCTION

THE BRONTË PARSONAGE MUSEUM is one of the great British literary shrines, attracting visitors from all over the world to the home of the famous family. The Brontë siblings moved to the Georgian parsonage when their father, the Reverend Patrick Brontë, was installed as perpetual curate in the Yorkshire hilltop village of Haworth in 1820. Soon after, they lost their mother Maria and, in 1825, two elder sisters, and were cared for by their mother's sister, their Cornish Aunt Branwell. In this house, surrounded by high moorland, the three remaining sisters, Charlotte, Emily and Anne, and their brother Branwell, grew up together, reading widely and showing great promise even in their juvenile writing.

Here they wrote their remarkable novels, including *Jane Eyre*, *Wuthering Heights* and *The Tenant of Wildfell Hall*, and here they died tragically young, Emily in 1848, aged 30, and Charlotte in 1855, aged 38. Anne also died young, in Scarborough in 1849, aged 29. The enduring popularity of their books, an influence on so many authors and the inspiration for numerous cinema and television adaptations, has ensured that the Brontës have remained in print ever since. Publication of Elizabeth Gaskell's *Life of Charlotte Brontë* in 1857 generated more

BELOW: Charlotte's copy of a portrait of **Mrs Brontë**. Cornish-born Maria Branwell married Patrick Brontë in December 1812 and died in 1821, only a year after the family's move to Haworth.

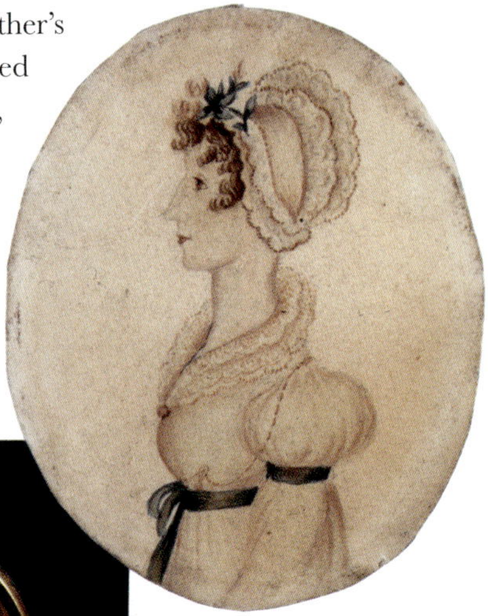

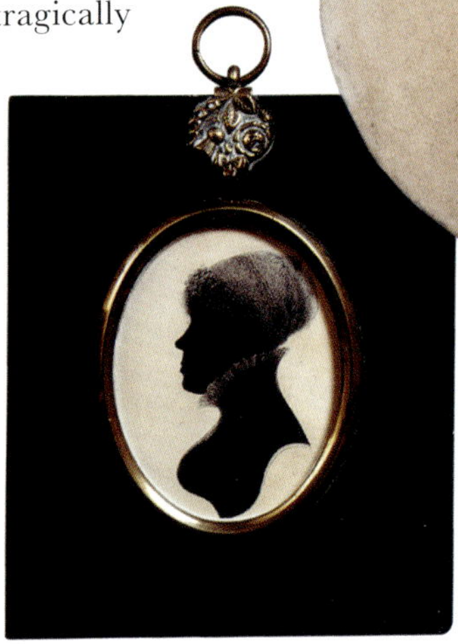

LEFT: **Elizabeth Branwell**, Maria's unmarried sister, moved to Yorkshire from Penzance after Maria's death to care for the Brontë children.

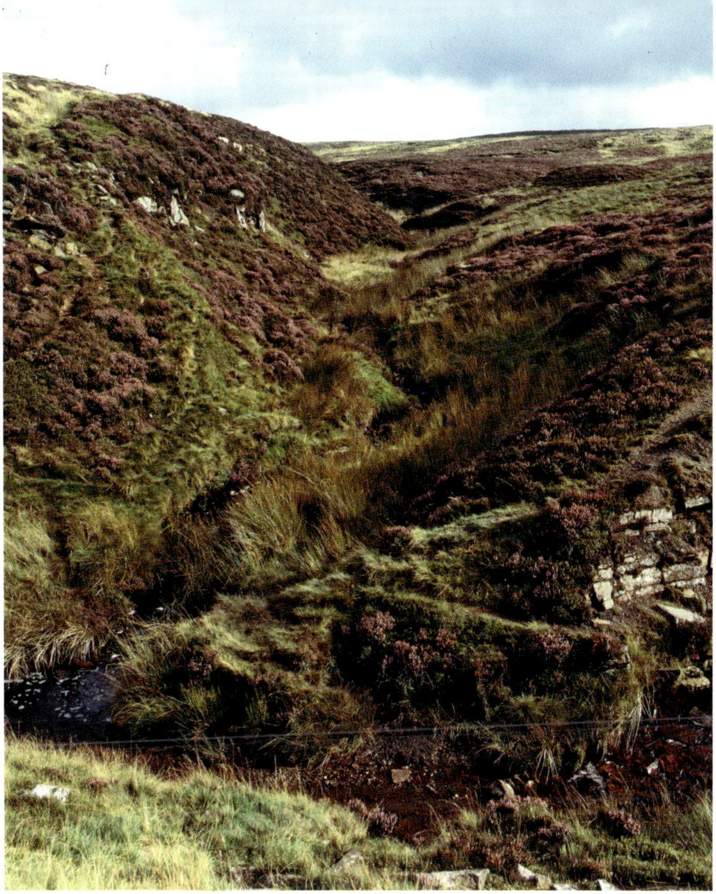

The rough windswept **moorland landscape** which surrounds Haworth was a source of inspiration to all the Brontës, featuring most notably in Emily's *Wuthering Heights*.

interest, and the fame of the talented siblings grew. Visitors began to arrive in Haworth even during Charlotte's lifetime, to see the landscape which inspired the novels, and after her death this developed into a form of literary tourism. Her father Patrick sometimes welcomed those paying their respects, but his successor, the Reverend John Wade, discouraged them. In the late nineteenth and early twentieth centuries, it was common for visitors to travel from all over the world without being able to see inside the Brontë family home. From 1895, however, Brontë memorabilia was on display at the Brontë Society's first museum, in rented rooms above the Yorkshire Penny Bank in Haworth.

In 1927 the Church of England offered the Parsonage for sale, and it was bought by Sir James Roberts, self-made Haworth textiles manufacturer and owner of Salts Mill, for £3000 and presented to the Brontë Society, together with £500 to pay for conversion into a museum and library. Today visitors to the Brontës' home experience period recreations of the rooms where the sisters wrote, cooked, and slept, and can view the world-famous collection of manuscripts, books and art. When the Brontë Parsonage Museum opened, however, the collection was displayed in cases in the dining room, and a custodian lived on site in the area that is now the Bonnell Room and the exhibition room above it.

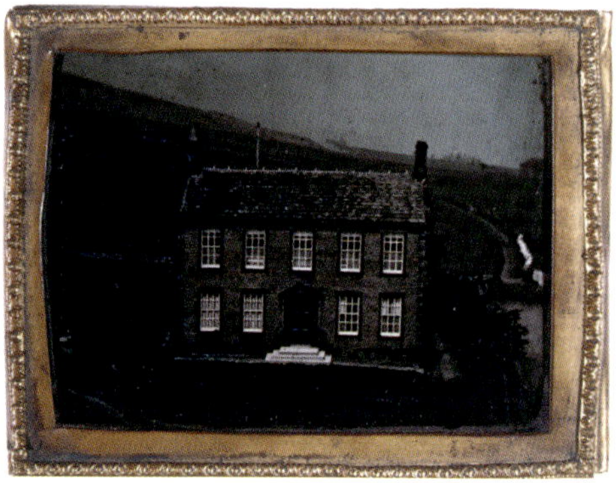

An early ambrotype photograph of the Parsonage shows it in its moorland setting.

By the outbreak of the Second World War the Museum had 9000 visitors a year, and it stayed open through the war. In 1947 visitor figures reached a staggering 53,000, fuelled by popular film adaptations of *Wuthering Heights*, starring Laurence Olivier and Merle Oberon (1939), *Jane Eyre*, starring Joan Fontaine and Orson Welles (1944), and *Devotion*, starring Olivia de Havilland as Charlotte Brontë (1946). During the 1950s the rooms were refurbished in an attempt to recreate their appearance in the early nineteenth century, using original furniture returned to the Brontë Society after being sold off at Patrick Brontë's death in 1861. The collection was displayed on the upper floor of the new wing added by Wade. In the 1980s, the upstairs display area was opened up to allow a better view of the world-class collection, and in 1989 all furniture not belonging to the Brontës was removed to leave only authentic items, with the exception of the reproduction bed in Patrick Brontë's bedroom, which is based on a drawing by Branwell.

Twenty-five years on, our latest major refurbishment is based on historic research and scientific investigation. The University of Lincoln analysed evidence found in the house, and historical interior

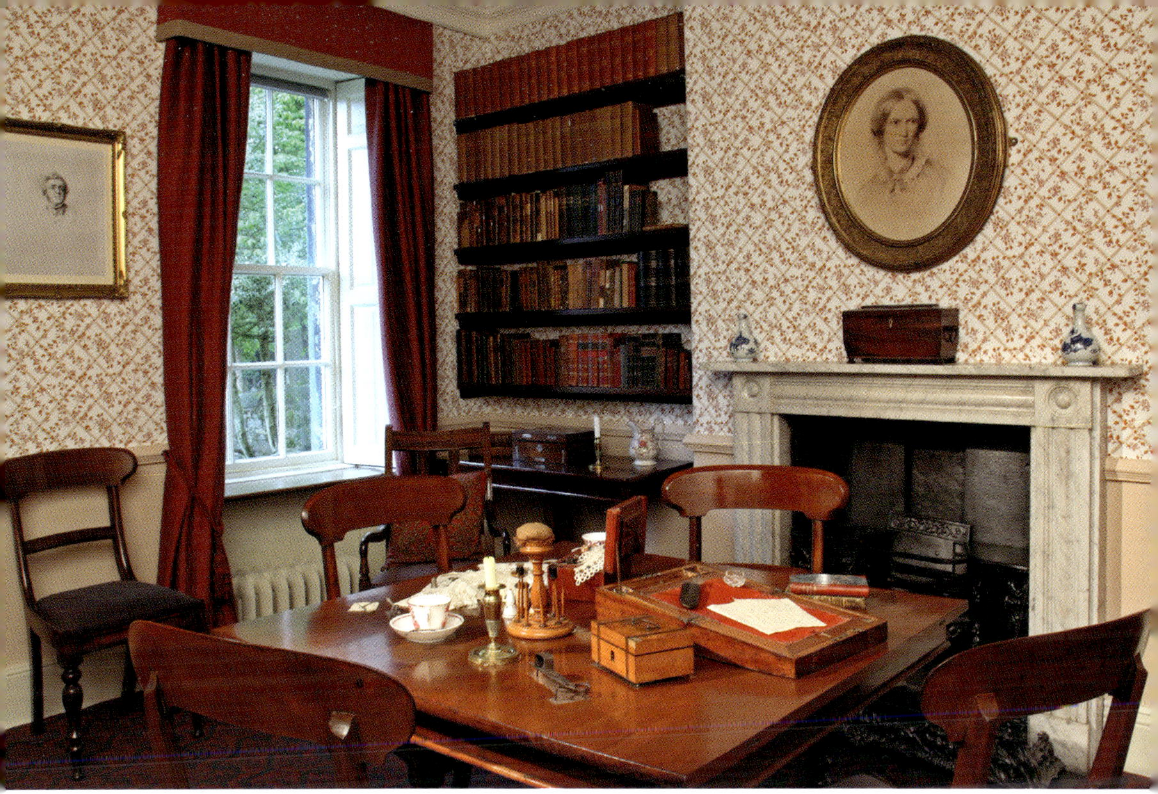

The **dining room**, where the sisters did most of their writing.

design consultant Allyson McDermott drew on those findings, together with a wide range of historic sources, including letters, inventory sales and contemporary watercolours, to produce a historically accurate scheme. The specially mixed paint colours, bespoke wallpapers and curtain fabrics of the dining room and study (the latter created from a store room for her new husband, the Reverend Arthur Bell Nicholls) particularly reflect Charlotte Brontë's decorative choices, paid for with income from sales of *Jane Eyre* (1847). Charlotte also re-decorated her father's study, but interestingly did not create one for herself, despite now being a renowned writer, preferring instead to continue writing at the dining-room table. She had the dining room enlarged, and ordered crimson curtains in union cloth, wallpaper and a carpet, all of which are now reproduced to match contemporary descriptions.

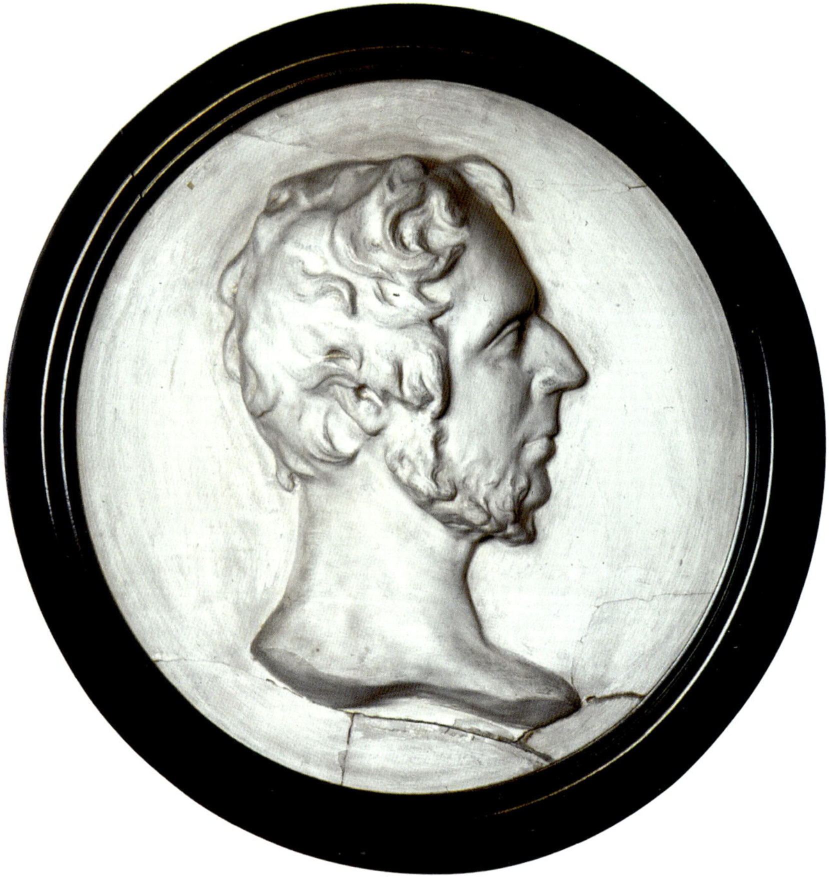

The paint colours seem extraordinarily modern; we now know that Charlotte had her own bedroom painted an unusual blue-green. The wallpapers, especially that in Branwell's study, are striking, but some rooms, for example the children's study and the kitchen, remain as simple as they would have been when the Brontës were growing up. Both rooms are washed in distemper and, as then, are regularly re-painted when they become dirty.

Plaster medallion by Joseph Bentley Leyland showing **Branwell Brontë** in profile.

Today a visit to the Brontë Parsonage Museum, now looking closer than ever to the way it did in the family's time, is a moving experience. But the Parsonage is not simply a re-creation of the Brontës' home – it is also a world-famous museum holding unique memorabilia, manuscripts, books and artworks inspired by their novels, and stills from film adaptations of their work, together with an extensive research library. Many of these artefacts are on display; still more are available to view by appointment in our library. The Parsonage Museum and adjoining meadow, where the Brontës dried their washing, are still run today by the Brontë Society, the world's oldest literary society. The Society encourages contemporary responses to the Brontës through creative writing, residencies and artistic interventions, organises lively lifelong learning events, and conducts an extensive schools programme, giving us all a chance to celebrate the Brontës' remarkable legacy.

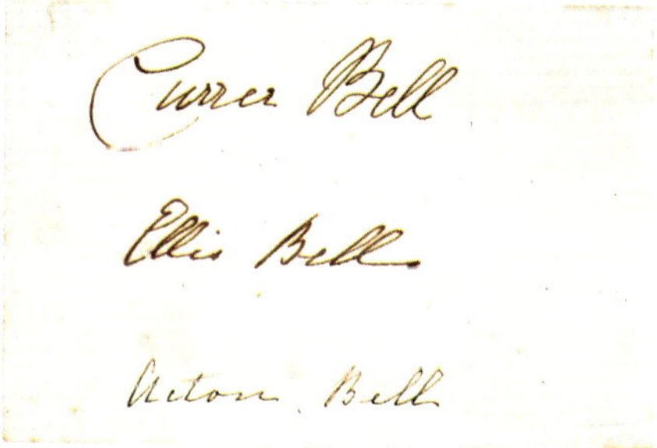

ABOVE: The **signatures** of Currer, Ellis and Acton Bell, the pseudonyms under which the three Brontë sisters published their work, provided by them for an early autograph hunter.

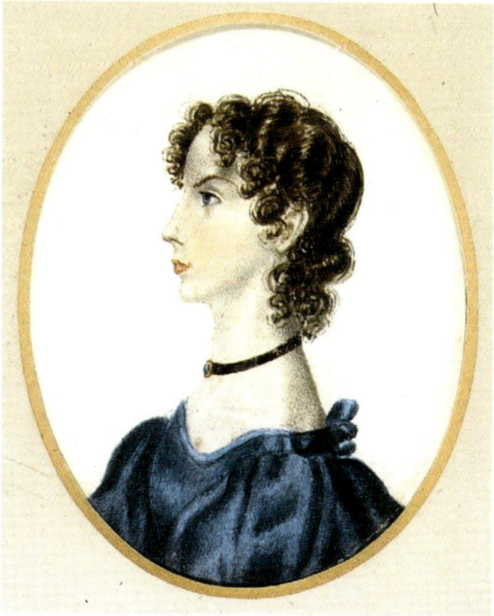

RIGHT: Watercolour of her **sister Anne** by Charlotte Brontë.

TOUR OF THE PARSONAGE
Entrance Hall

IN HER 1871 *Reminiscences*, Charlotte's close schoolfriend, Ellen Nussey, recalled her first visit to the Parsonage in the summer of 1833 and how, after family prayers at eight o'clock, Mr Brontë would lock and bar the front door at nine, '…always giving as he passed the sitting-room door a kindly admonition to the "children" not to be late; half-way up the stairs he stayed his steps to wind up the clock…' She added, 'The hall floor and stairs were done with sand-stone, always beautifully clean, as was everything about the house', and described the walls as being, 'not papered, but stained in a pretty dove-coloured tint'. Recent analysis has revealed that this colour was a pale blue/grey, which has been re-introduced to paint the entrance hall, stairwell and landing. The entrance hall would have been larger than it is today, as Charlotte widened the dining room at the expense of the hall when she had several structural alterations made to the building in 1850.

In a letter to a friend, Elizabeth Gaskell said: 'I don't know that I ever saw a spot more exquisitely clean… Everything fits into, and is in harmony with, the idea of a country parsonage, possessed by people of very moderate means.' The furnishings in the Parsonage reflect the simplicity of the late Georgian and early Victorian period. Ellen described the effect as 'scant and bare indeed' but nevertheless, 'mind and thought, I had almost said elegance but certainly refinement, diffused themselves over all, and made nothing really wanting.' Although Ellen stated that 'there was not much carpet anywhere', except in the dining room and Mr Brontë's study, a stair carpet and stair rods were sold at the 1861 sale, along with several other 'Kidderminster Carpets and Rugs'. Ellen also recalled that Mr Brontë was fearful that the combination of young children, candles and curtains would be a fire hazard. The windows were shuttered at night and curtains were introduced at a later date.

OPPOSITE: The elegant **entrance hall**, looking through a classic Georgian-style arch to the flight of sandstone stairs beyond.

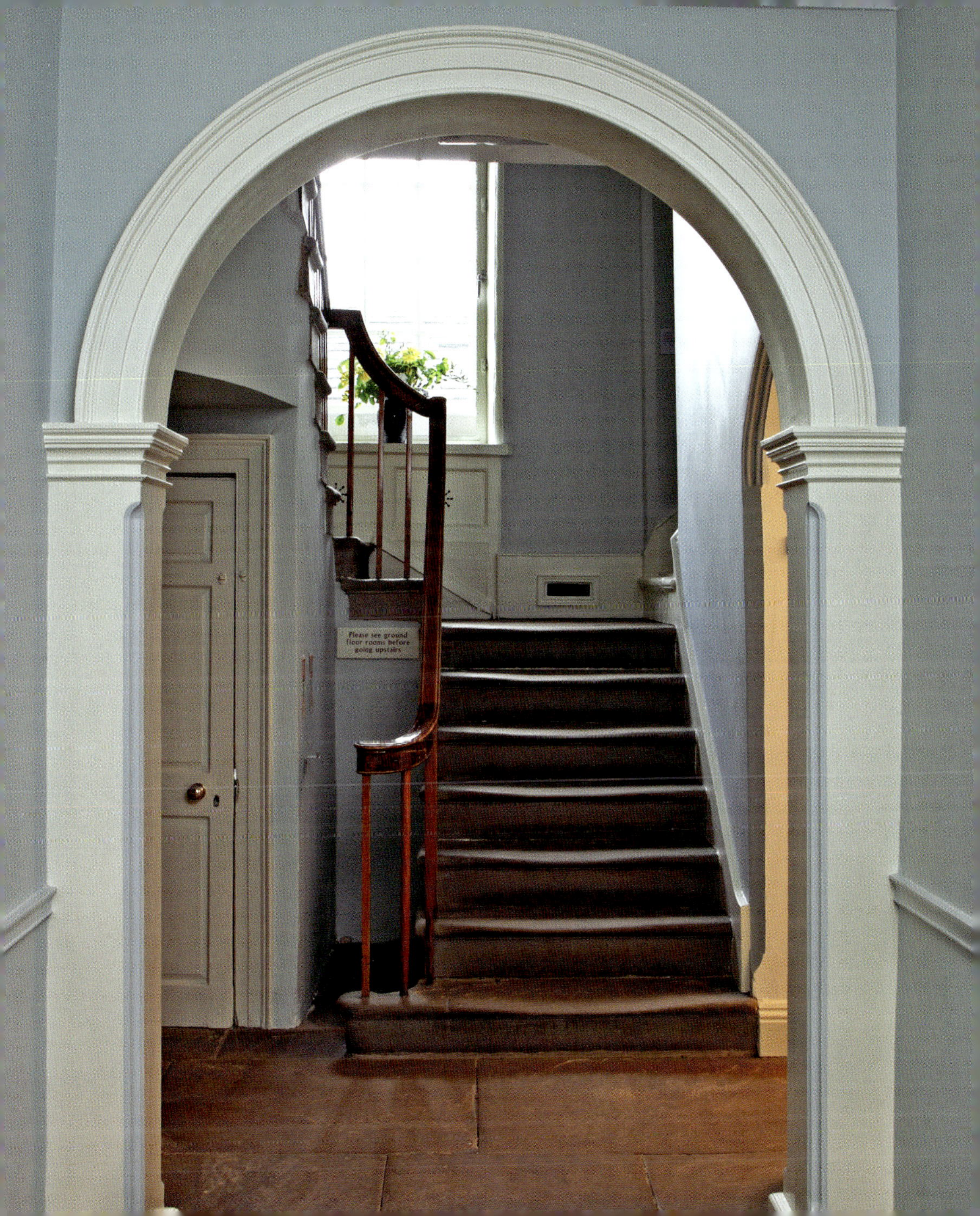
Please see ground
floor rooms before
going upstairs

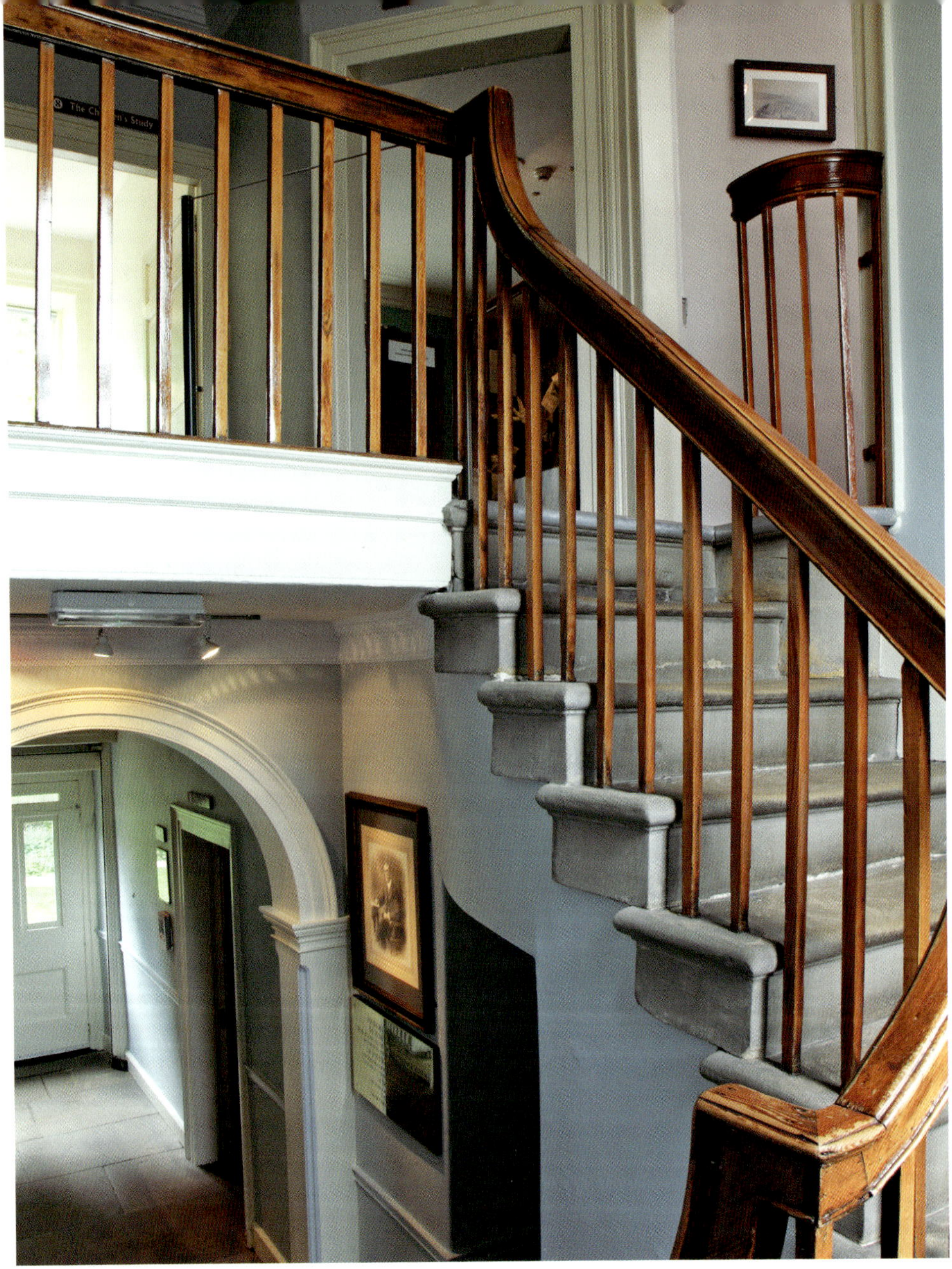

OPPOSITE: Looking back from the **landing halfway up the stairs** towards the hall and plaque commemorating the gift of the parsonage by Sir James Roberts.

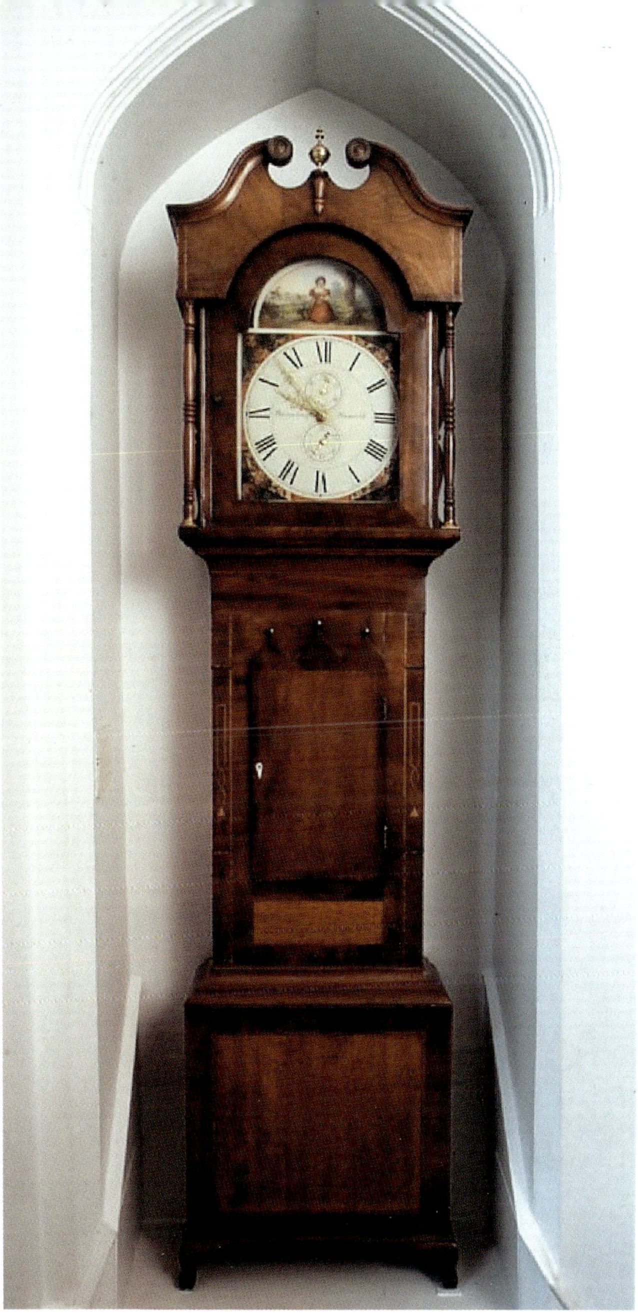

RIGHT: This mahogany **longcase clock**, made by Barraclough of Haworth, stands halfway up the stairs and was wound nightly by Mr Brontë.

Mr Brontë's Study

THE REVEREND PATRICK BRONTË carried out most of his parish business from this room, which he used as his study. In old age, he was described as 'sitting in a plain, uncushioned chair, upright as a soldier' before the fire. Elizabeth Gaskell did not know the young, enthusiastic Patrick Brontë, whose wife Maria addressed him as 'My Dear Saucy Pat' during their courtship; Gaskell did not encounter Mr Brontë until she visited her friend Charlotte at the Parsonage in 1853. By then he was in his seventies and in poor health, and had suffered the loss of all but one of his family. Thus Gaskell's sometimes unfavourable presentation of Mr Brontë misses the dimension of the young father whose lively ideas, discussion and encouragement stimulated and informed the minds of his children.

Mr Brontë was a remarkable clergyman; deeply concerned about the welfare of his parishioners, he founded a Sunday school and campaigned for improvements in sanitation in Haworth. He was keenly aware of wider religious and political issues and wrote many letters to the newspapers. As a Church of England clergyman, Mr Brontë did not support the strict Calvinist doctrine of only the 'elect' reaching Heaven and his attitude tended rather towards the more generous message of forgiveness and hope.

Mr Brontë's eyesight deteriorated with age until he was almost blind. When he was 69 he travelled to Manchester for a cataract operation without anaesthetic, which improved his sight, although he continued to wear spectacles and to use a magnifying glass to help him to read. It was while Charlotte was nursing her father in their lodgings in Manchester that she began to write *Jane Eyre*.

It was in this room that Patrick Brontë first discovered that his eldest daughter was a successful author. In a letter of August 1850,

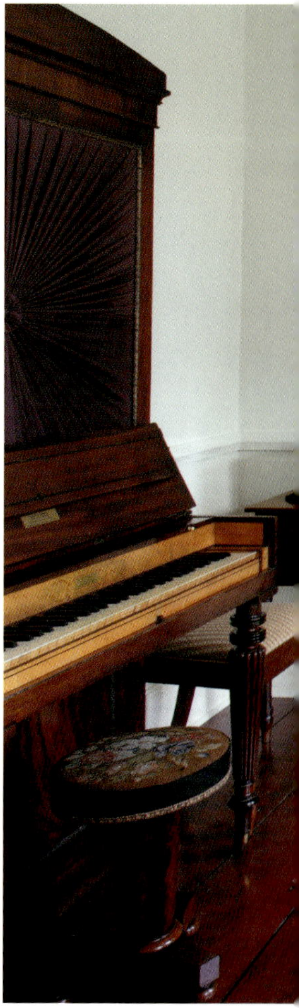

General view of **Mr Brontë's study**, the focus of his demanding parish duties. Branwell's copy of a work by John Martin hangs above the fireplace.

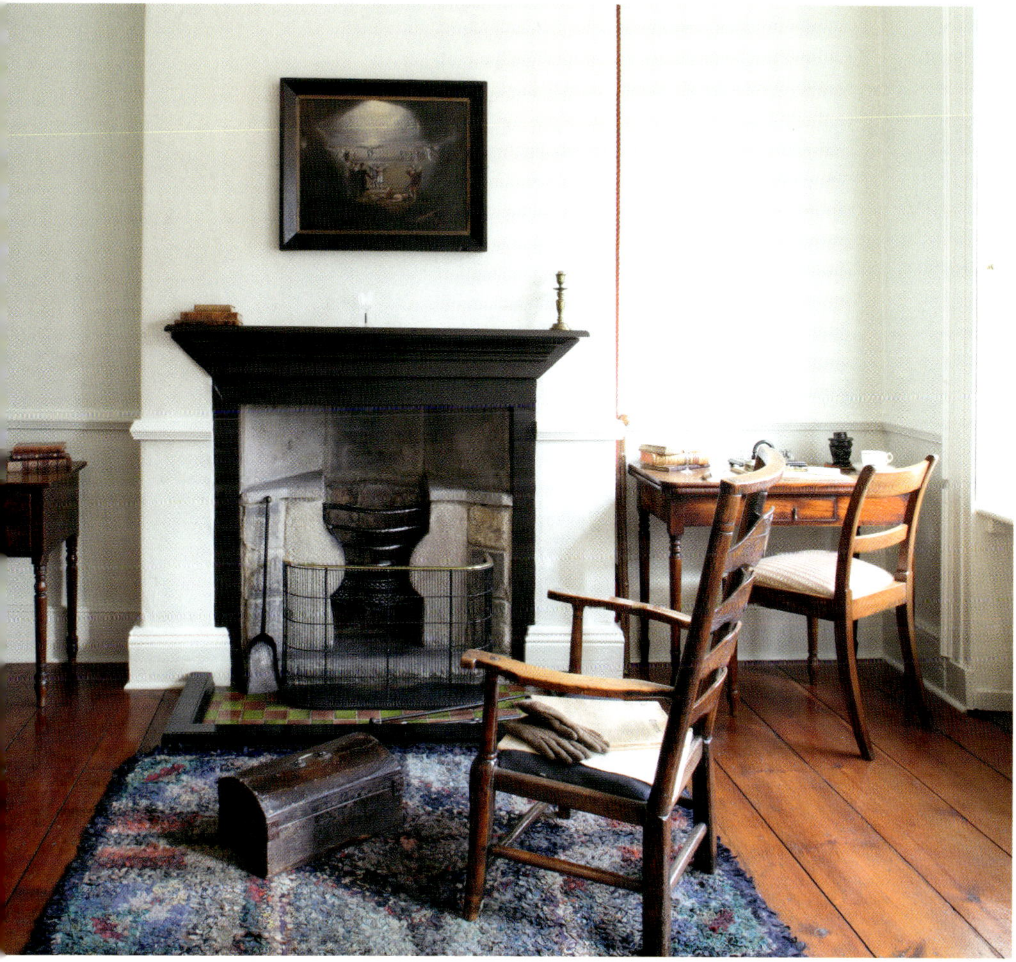

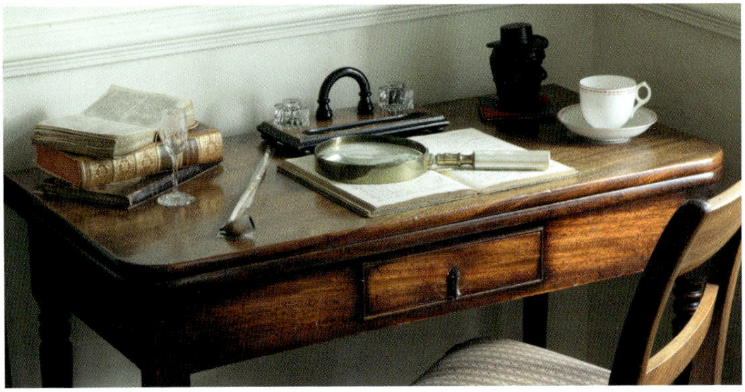

LEFT: In later life Mr Brontë suffered from failing eyesight, as indicated by the **magnifying glass** on his study table.

BELOW: Mr Brontë bought this **'cabinet' piano** for his children; the strings are arranged vertically so that the piano takes up less space.

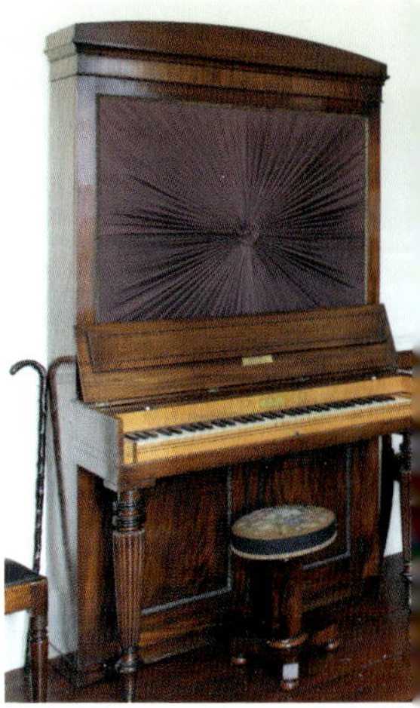

Elizabeth Gaskell recounts the following exchange when Charlotte, carrying a copy of *Jane Eyre* and some reviews, marched into her father's study:

'"Papa, I've been writing a book." "Have you my dear?" and he went on reading. "But Papa, I want you to look at it." "I can't be troubled to read MS." "But it is printed." "I hope you have not been involving yourself in any such silly expense." "I think I shall gain some money by it. May I read you some reviews?"'

Later that day, he announced: '"Children, Charlotte has been writing a book – and I think it is a better one than I expected."' Mr Brontë was always very proud of his children's achievements, attributing their ability in part to his own eccentricity. He had fought his way from a humble background in Ireland to Cambridge University and knew the value of education, fostering his children's interest in art, literature, politics and music. Three popular engravings of biblical scenes by the Romantic painter and engraver John Martin (1789-1854) hung in this room: *The Deluge*, *Belshazzar's Feast* and *Joshua Commanding the Sun*. Martin's dramatic, large-scale pictures were an early inspiration for the young Brontës, and Branwell's copy of Martin's *Jacob's Dream* hangs above the fireplace. There is no evidence that this room was ever papered, and it has been painted in simple off-white distemper.

OPPOSITE: This **portrait of Mr Brontë** as a young man, by an unknown artist, depicts the lively and intelligent man whose encouragement helped to inspire his children's creativity.

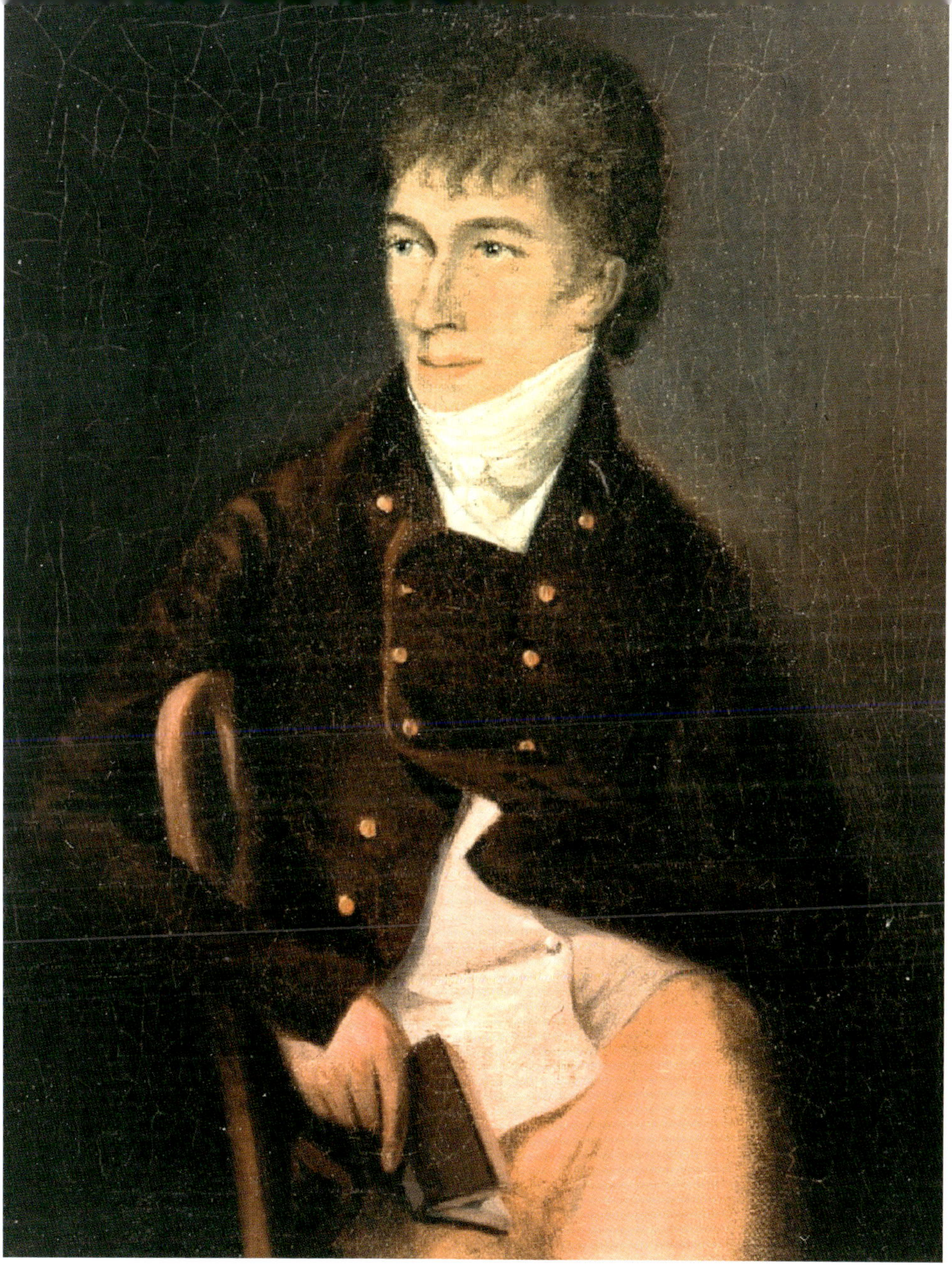

Dining Room

CHARLOTTE, EMILY AND ANNE did most of their writing here, and the room was the focus of their creativity. *Jane Eyre*, *Wuthering Heights* and *Agnes Grey* were written in this room. It was the sisters' habit to walk around the table every evening until about eleven o'clock, reading and discussing their writing plans and projects. After the deaths of Emily and Anne, Charlotte walked in solitude, unable to sleep without this nightly ritual. Martha Brown, servant at the Parsonage, described how, 'My heart aches to hear Miss Brontë walking, walking on alone.'

The dining room would also have been used to entertain visitors, and therefore it is the room most often described in articles and contemporary accounts. Like the bedroom directly above, this room was enlarged by Charlotte in 1850.

The dining room, sometimes called the parlour, is furnished in a simple style. Elizabeth Gaskell said, 'The parlour has evidently been refurbished within the last few years, since Miss Brontë's success has enabled her to have a little more money to spend…The prevailing colour of the room is crimson…There is her likeness by Richmond, an engraving from Lawrence's picture of Thackeray, and two recesses, on each side of the high, narrow, old-fashioned mantel-piece, filled with books.' The books now on the shelves are of the period, while those owned by the Brontës themselves are stored securely elsewhere. Charlotte's decorative scheme from the early 1850s has been reintroduced. Analysis

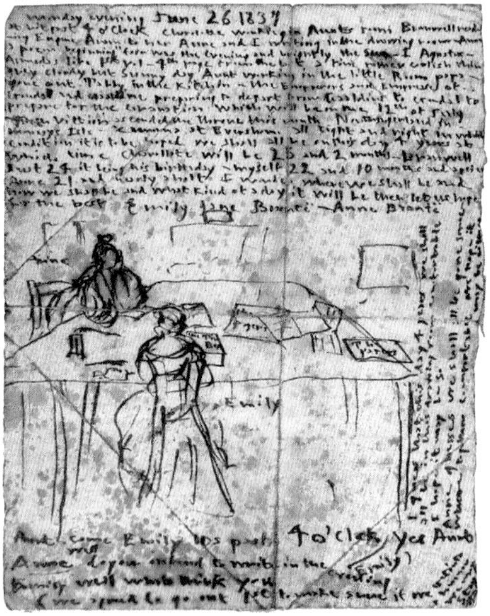

Emily's diary paper of 26 June 1837, which includes a sketch of two female figures labelled 'Anne' and 'Emily' seated at the dining-room table, with the diary papers they wrote every four years, and the tin box that contained them, scattered on the table.

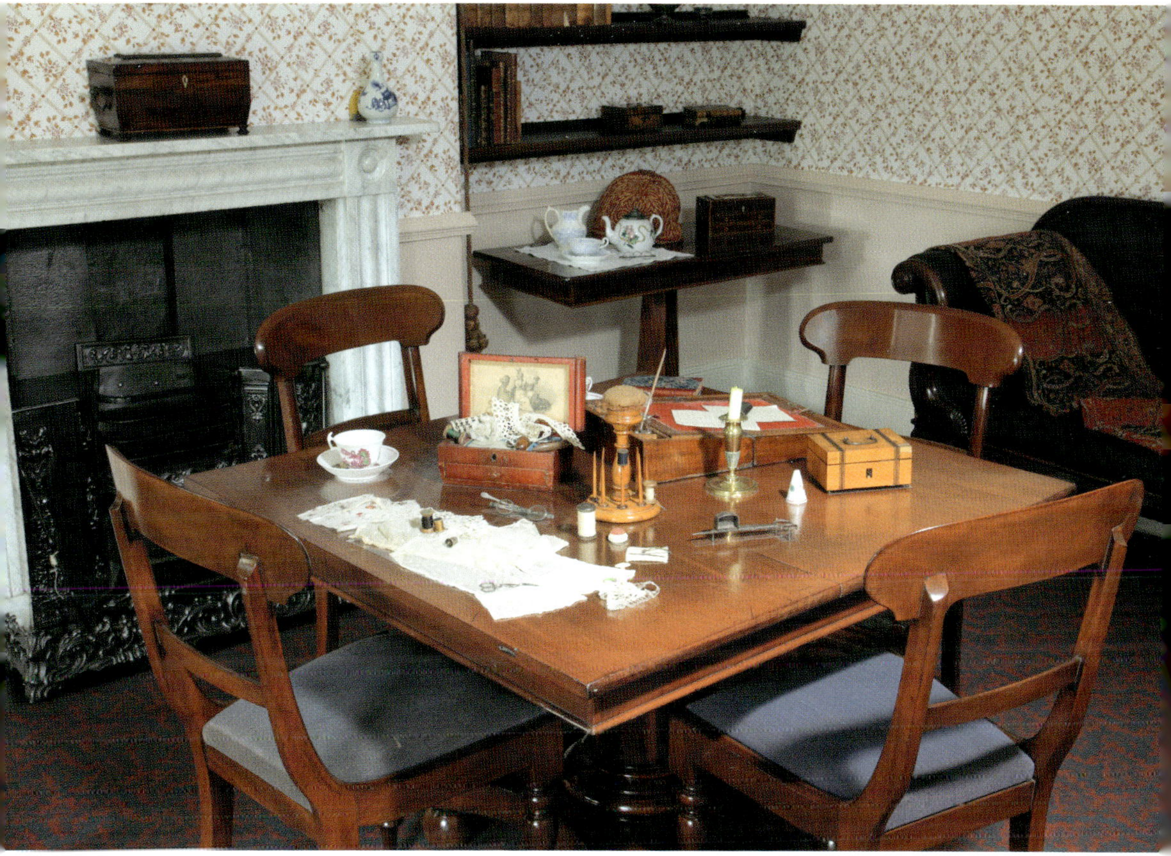

The **pedestal table** now displayed in the dining room was made for the Brontës by the Haworth joiner, William Wood, and was sold along with the rest of the furniture on Patrick's death in 1861.

has revealed that the dining room was papered both before and after Charlotte's alterations, and so the paper chosen is a contemporary design, in scarlet to match the curtains, which in turn have been specially woven in crimson union cloth, just as Charlotte ordered.

Charlotte recalled little about her mother, who died in 1821 when Charlotte was just five years old, but she retained a treasured, vague memory of Mrs Brontë nursing Branwell in this room.

Kitchen

'ONE NIGHT about the time when the cold sleet and dreary fogs of November are succeeded by the snow storms & high peircing nightwinds of confirmed winter we where all sitting round the warm blazing kitchen fire having just concluded a quarel with Taby concerning the propriety of lighting a candle…' Charlotte Brontë, *Tales of the Islanders*, 31 June 1829.

As children, the Brontës would gather round the kitchen fire to listen to their servant Tabby's dark tales of the Yorkshire moors. The sisters were expected to take their share of the household tasks, and the kitchen features in many of their surviving accounts of daily life at the Parsonage. After Aunt Branwell's death in 1842, Emily acted as housekeeper, helping in the kitchen and baking bread.

Following Patrick Brontë's death in 1861, the Parsonage became the home of the Reverend John Wade, who made several alterations to the house, particularly to the kitchen. A back kitchen, where the washing and heavier household work was carried out in the Brontës' time, was demolished to make way for a large kitchen extension, blocking the mullioned window which had formerly looked out towards the moors. The range was removed, and the old kitchen became a passageway to Wade's new dining room in the large gabled wing that he added. Today the kitchen houses displays of furniture and utensils which belonged to the Brontë family. A kitchen range of the correct period has been added, to help recreate the room's original appearance, and the walls have been washed in distemper, as they would have been during the Brontës' time.

OPPOSITE: **The kitchen range**, is of the correct period.

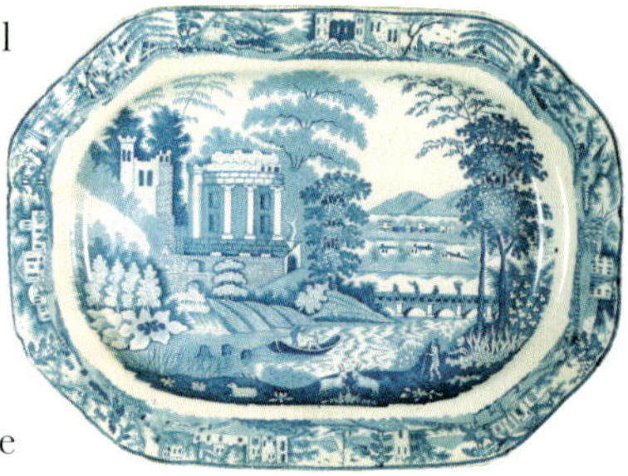

ABOVE: Blue and white **meat platter**.

BELOW: Brown glazed **teapot**, commemorating Mr Brontë's predecessor at Haworth church, William Grimshaw.

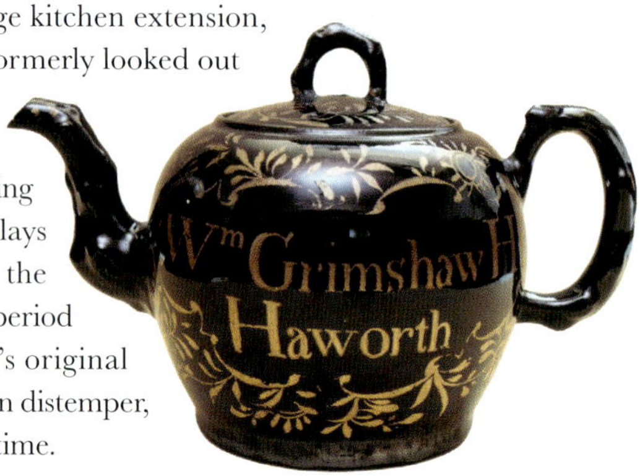

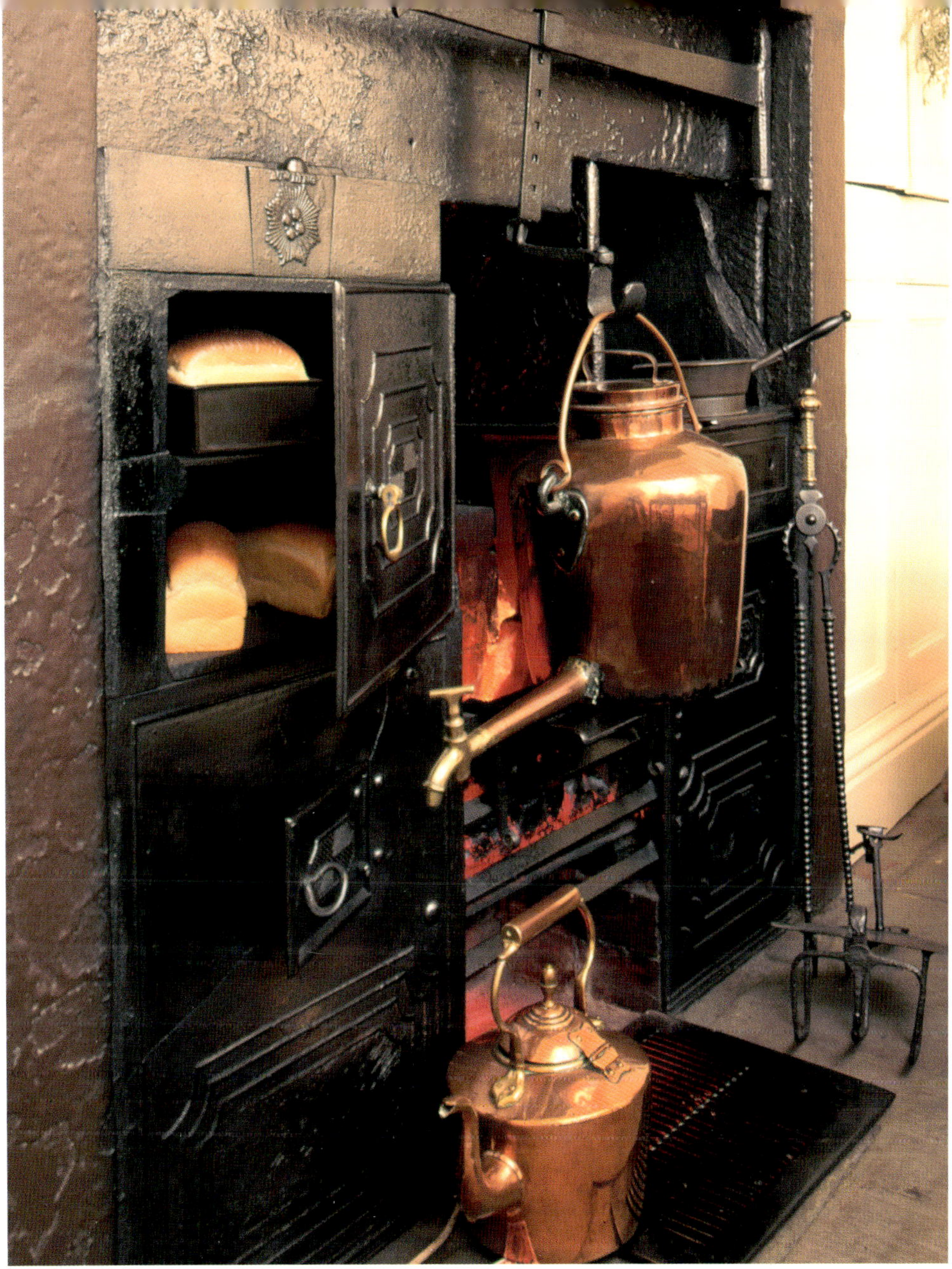

Mr Nicholls' Study

ACCORDING TO ELIZABETH GASKELL, this room was originally 'a sort of flagged store-room', probably used for fuel, which could only be reached from the outside. Before her marriage in 1854, Charlotte converted the room into a study for her future husband, the Reverend Arthur Bell Nicholls, who in 1845 had come to assist her father as curate at Haworth. A fireplace was added to the room and the present doorway into the entrance hall was created. Charlotte died within a year of her marriage, and Mr Nicholls remained at the Parsonage to care for the elderly Patrick Brontë and to assist in the performance of his pastoral duties. On Patrick's death in 1861, Mr Nicholls returned to his native Ireland, taking with him many mementos of the Brontë family. He died in 1906 aged 88, having survived Charlotte by 51 years.

Describing her preparations for the room's conversion in a letter dated 22 May 1854, Charlotte wrote: '...I have been very busy stitching – the little new room is got into order now and the green and white curtains are up – they exactly suit the papering and look neat and clean enough.' A sample of wallpaper, held in the New York Public Library, is authenticated by Elizabeth Gaskell in an accompanying note, which describes it as being a 'Slip of the paper with which Charlotte Brontë papered her future husband's study, before they were married'. This wallpaper has been reproduced and used in this room, with curtains in a complementary green-patterned fabric of the period. Forensic evi-

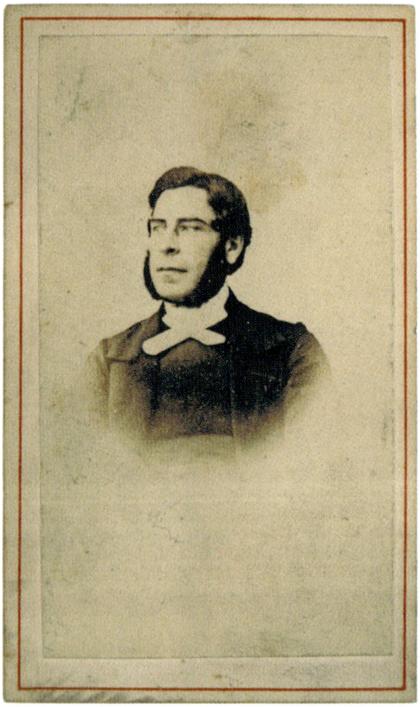

Photograph of **Arthur Bell Nicholls**, who came to Haworth as curate in 1845 and married Charlotte in 1854.

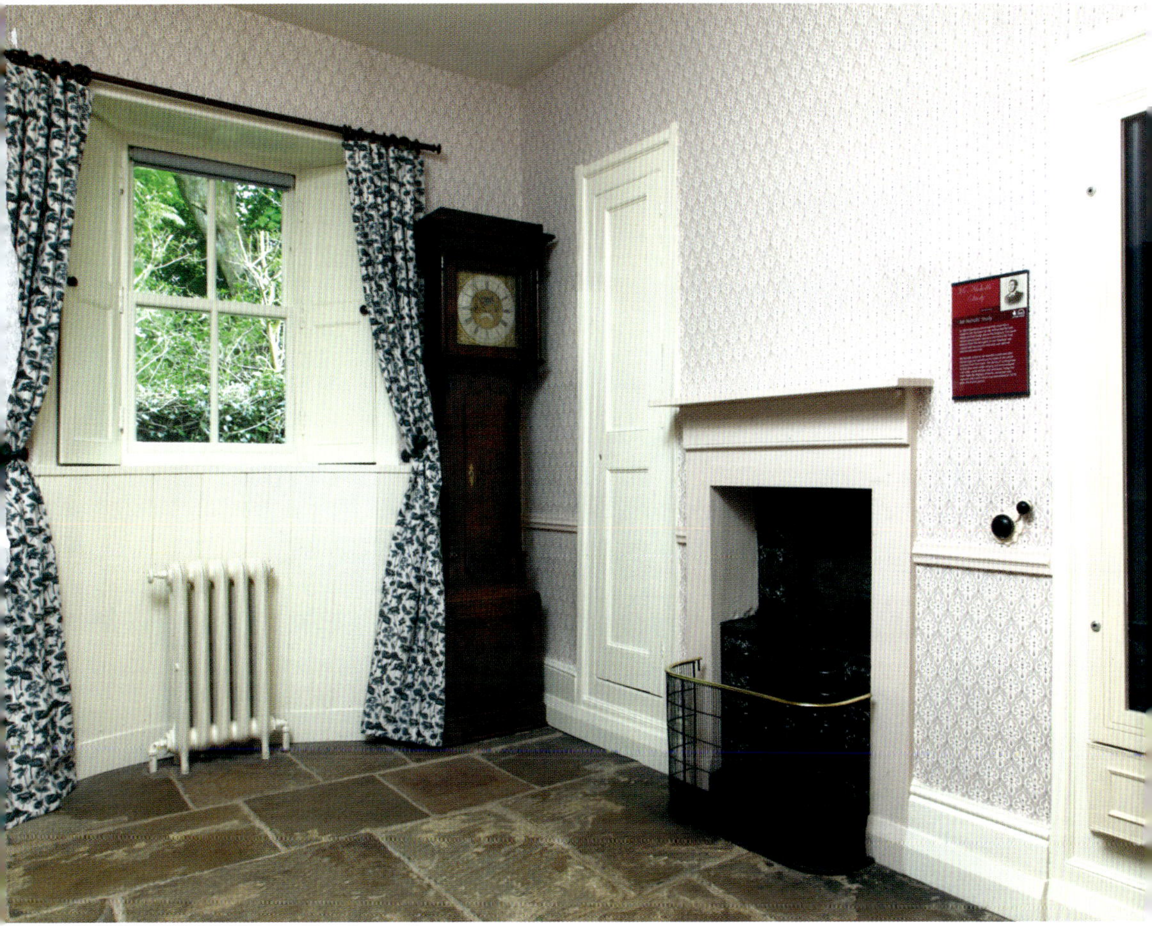

This room was converted by Charlotte to make a study for her future husband; several relics from Haworth Old Church are now displayed in it.

dence showed that, before Charlotte's alterations, the room had only ever been decorated twice, with an off-white distemper.

Today the room is used to display artefacts relating to Arthur Bell Nicholls and to Haworth Old Church, where he served as curate from 1845 to 1861.

Servant's Room

Martha Brown, who came to the Parsonage in 1839 and remained until Mr Brontë's death in 1861.

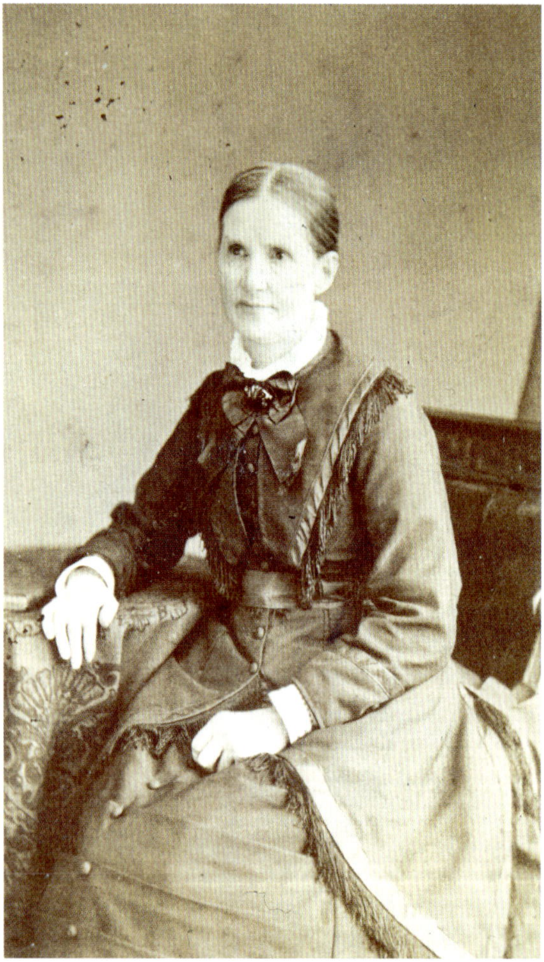

ALTHOUGH WE DO NOT know exactly where the Brontë family slept all of the time, there was always at least one live-in servant, and this was her bedroom. For 30 years the Brontës were served by a local woman, Tabby Aykroyd, who came to work at the Parsonage when she was in her fifties. Tabby was described in *The Life of Charlotte Brontë* as a 'thorough specimen of a Yorkshire woman of her class, in dialect, in appearance, and in character…Her words were far from flattery; but she would spare no deeds in the cause of those whom she kindly regarded.' Tabby must have been a comforting presence to the motherless Brontë children; she became more of a family friend than a servant, and died in 1855 at the age of 84, just a few weeks before Charlotte. Martha Brown, the sexton's daughter, came to the Parsonage aged 11 to assist Tabby. She also remained with the family for many years and both women are buried in the churchyard, close to the Parsonage garden wall.

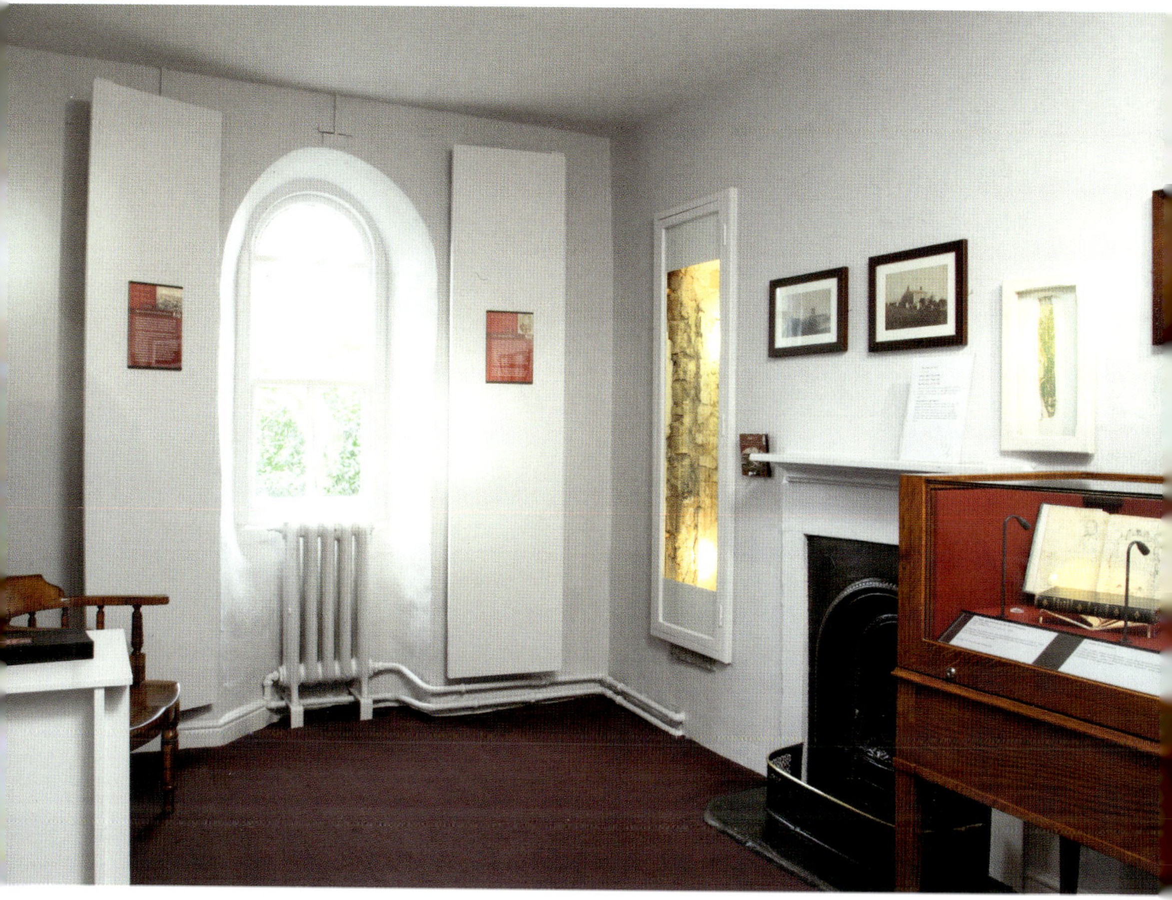

The **servant's room** used by both Tabby Aykroyd and Martha Brown; the mullioned window seen here was probably blocked in the time of the Brontës.

A recess in the wall, possibly once used as a cupboard, has been partly uncovered. Also visible is part of a mullioned window which was probably blocked up in the Brontës' time, during alterations to the house. Scientific analysis has shown that a grey paint covered the walls during the Brontë period, and this colour has been reproduced as closely as possible.

Charlotte's Room

THIS WAS THE MAIN BEDROOM, used by different members of the family over the years, depending on who happened to be at home at any particular time. In the nineteenth century it was more common for people to share rooms, and beds, than it is today. The room was enlarged at the expense of the little room over the hall in 1850. The unusual blue-green colour on the walls is an exact match for the colour we know to have been used here in the early 1850s.

Charlotte's room was the main bedroom and was used initially by her parents, but now displays a selection of memorabilia associated with Charlotte.

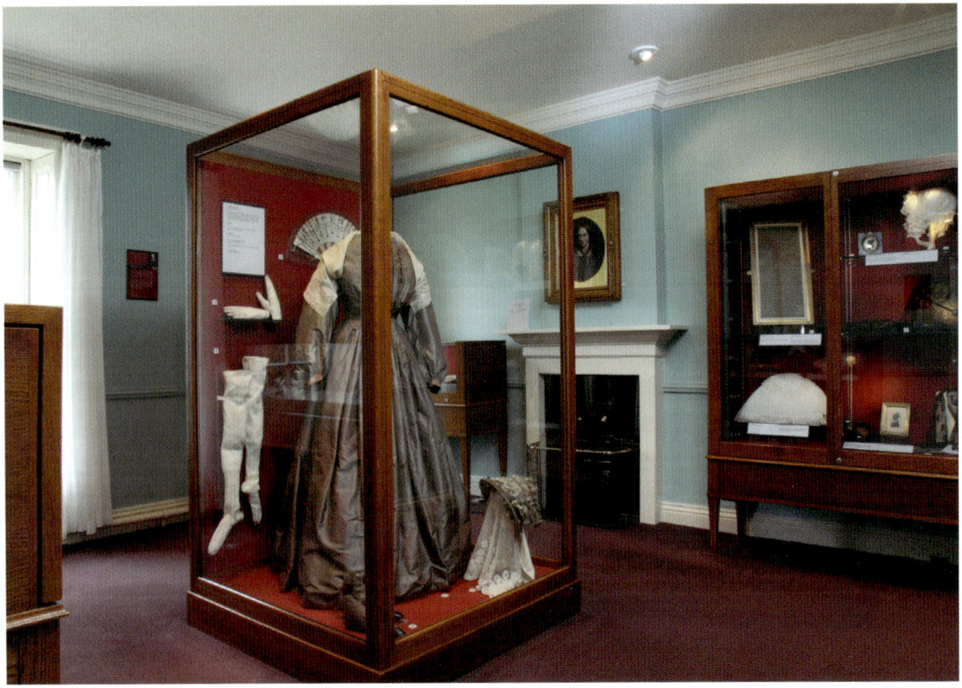

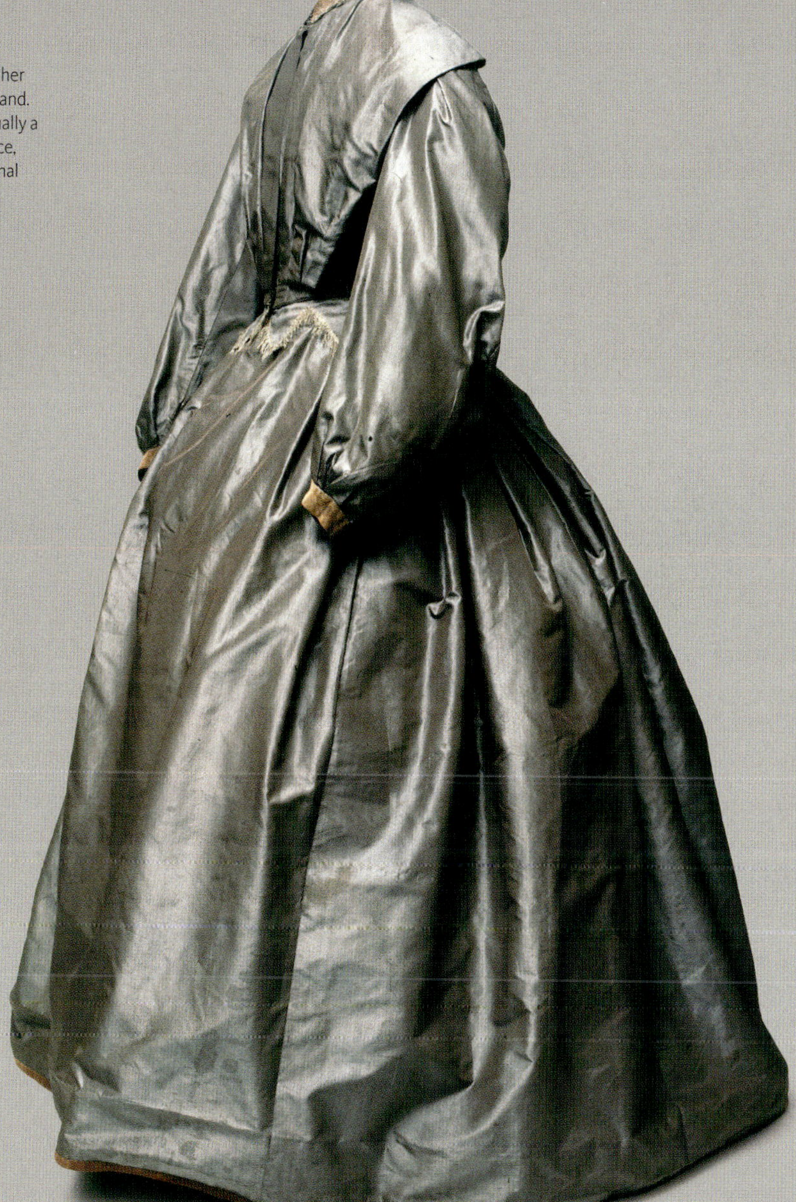

This **dress** was worn by Charlotte to set out on her honeymoon tour in Ireland. The dress, which is actually a separate skirt and bodice, has faded from its original striped lavender colour.

Initially, this was Patrick and Maria's room. Maria Brontë died here on 15 September 1821, aged 38. During her painful illness (probably cancer), she seldom complained, and Elizabeth Gaskell described how she would beg her nurse to 'raise her in bed to let her see her clean the grate, "because she did it as it was done in Cornwall".' After Mrs Brontë's death, her sister, Aunt Branwell, moved into this room and Patrick Brontë occupied the room opposite. At this time Anne was still a baby, and is likely to have slept here with her aunt during much of her early childhood. When Aunt Branwell died in 1842, Emily returned from Brussels, where she and Charlotte had both taken teaching posts, and remained at the Parsonage acting as housekeeper.

BELOW: **Portrait of Charlotte**, based on one by the well-known artist, George Richmond, and painted after Charlotte's death by J.H. Thompson, a friend of Branwell's.

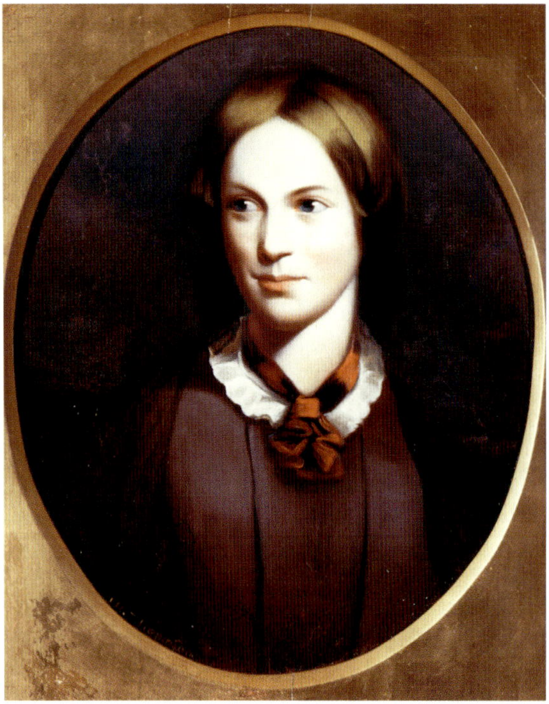

Charlotte returned permanently from Brussels in early 1844 and may have taken over the room then. Anne left her governessing duties at Thorp Green Hall, near York, in June 1845 and probably shared with either Charlotte or Emily from this point onwards. After the deaths of her sisters, Charlotte occupied this room alone, moving out occasionally if guests such as Elizabeth Gaskell came to stay. When Charlotte married, she and her husband shared the room and Charlotte died here on 31 March 1855, aged 38. Elizabeth Gaskell described how the gravely ill Charlotte overheard her husband praying beside her: '"Oh!" she whispered forth, "I am not going to die, am I? He will not separate us, we have been so happy."'

OPPOSITE: In this **illustrated letter** of March 1843 from Brussels, Charlotte, who was painfully aware of what she regarded as her plain appearance, has caricatured herself (bottom left) as an ugly, dwarfish figure.

48

Remember me to [redacted] & your Mother, tell me if any chances & changes have happened — remember me also to Mrs [redacted] when you see her —

You do no merit that I should prolong this letter — Good-bye to you dear Nell when I say so — it seems to me that you will hardly hear me — all the ~~heaving~~ waves of the Channel, heaving & roaring between must deaden the sound —

Good-bye

C B

J. Horsfall Turner

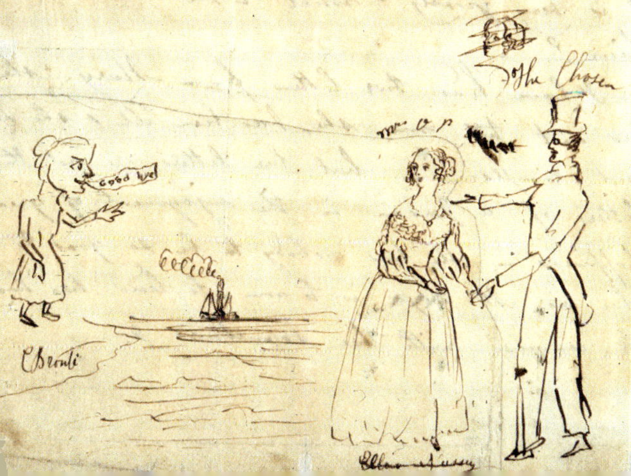

Dear N
ict I d
ffers of a
wail my
time of c
with oc
I have to
I ought
be than
hope I w
lways k
lonely or
or whatev
well — t
are
for whom
nd of co
nor even
eturned th
room my
whenever
oom — to
day time

Children's Study

THIS LITTLE ROOM is particularly associated with the Brontës as children, and later became Emily's bedroom. The room was simply decorated in distemper, and originally would have been wider, with room for a full-sized bed across the window, as shown in Emily's diary paper sketch, but it was affected by the enlargement of Charlotte's room in 1850.

According to Elizabeth Gaskell, the servants called the room the 'children's study' because it was here that, as young children, the Brontë siblings would act out their plays and write in their handmade 'little books'. The room may have been used by Branwell at some point, as the only boy, but is usually associated with Emily.

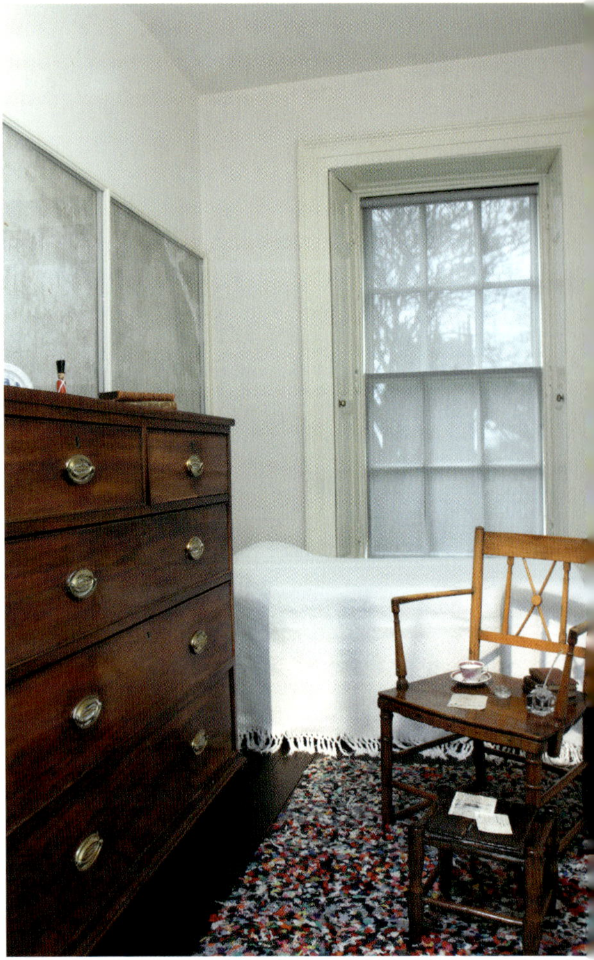

The children's study, now reduced in size due to alterations made by Charlotte.

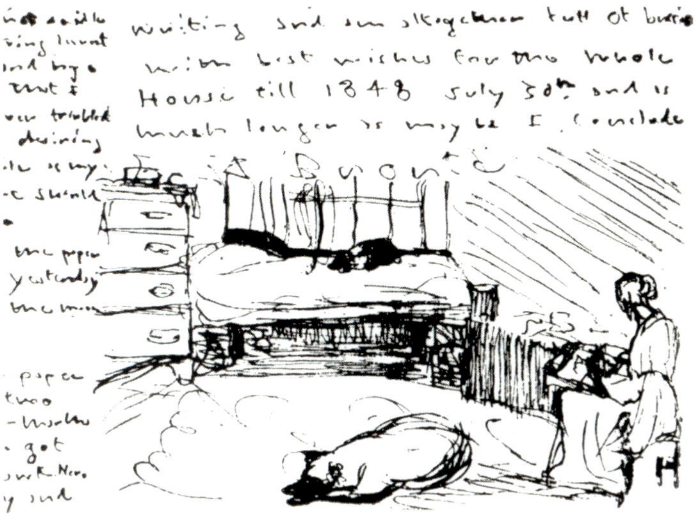

RIGHT: **Emily's diary paper sketch** from 1845, showing her writing in the room before its alteration, with her mastiff Keeper at her feet. The chest and stool shown in the sketch are displayed in the room.

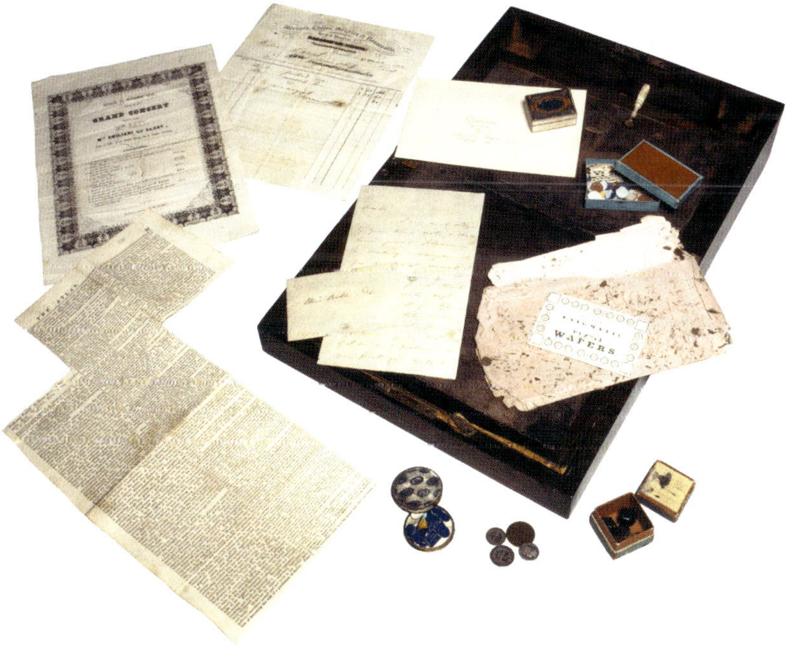

RIGHT: Each of the Brontë sisters owned her own **portable writing desk**; this one belonged to Emily and is made of rosewood, inlaid with mother-of-pearl. The contents have been preserved as Emily left them and include five reviews of *Wuthering Heights*, sealing wafers, blobs of sealing wax, pen shafts and nibs and a small envelope containing 'Clarke's enigmatic puzzle wafers' – small gummed labels for sealing envelopes which are printed with various acrostics.

Mr Brontë's Bedroom

AFTER THE DEATH of his wife in 1821, Patrick Brontë left the room they had shared and moved into the bedroom across the landing, which remained his for the rest of his life.

Patrick had lived through periods of Luddite and Chartist violence, to which clergymen often fell victim, and as a result would place a loaded pistol beside his bed at night, discharging the bullet by firing it from his bedroom window across the graveyard every morning.

In later years, Branwell's addiction to alcohol and opium made him a danger both to himself and his family. Mary Robinson, an early

OPPOSITE: Patrick Brontë moved to this room after his wife's death, sharing it with Branwell during the latter's last year.

BELOW: Very little of the Brontës' bedroom furniture survives; this half-tester bed is a reproduction, based on a sketch made by Branwell.

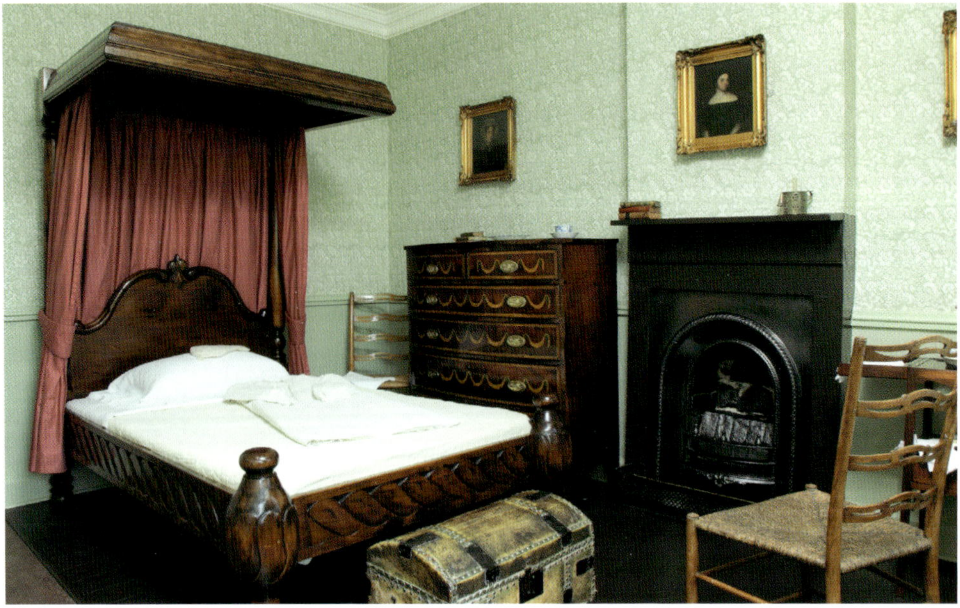

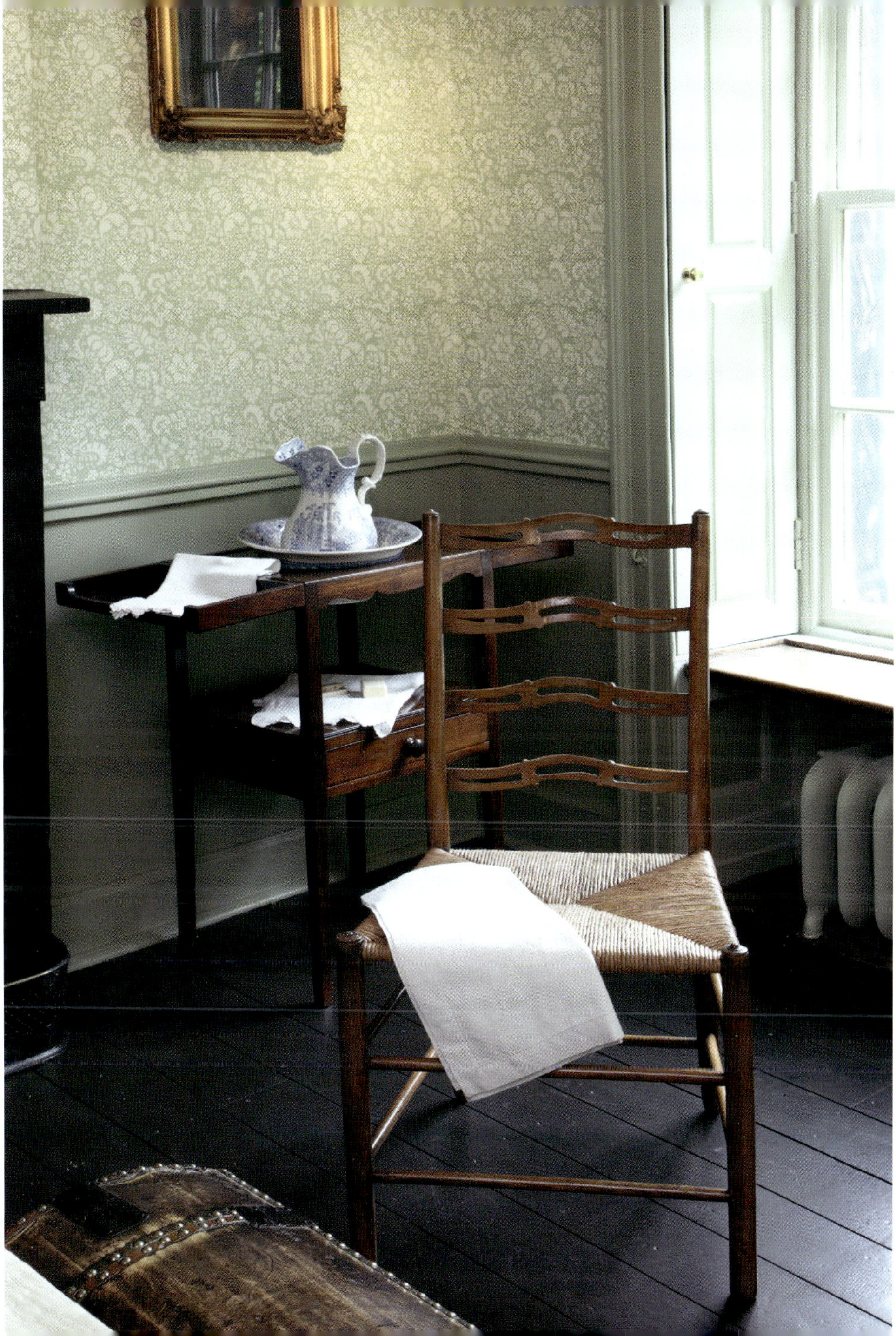

biographer, was told that on one occasion Branwell, stupefied with alcohol, set his bed on fire and was rescued by Emily. Whether true or not, the fear of such incidents led Mr Brontë to share his room with Branwell, in order to watch over him. Elizabeth Gaskell, writing of this period in the Brontës' lives, said of Branwell: 'For some time before his death he had attacks of delirium tremens of the most frightful character; he slept in his father's room, and he would sometimes declare that either he or his father should be dead before morning… In the mornings young Brontë would saunter out, saying, with a drunkard's incontinence of speech, "The poor old man and I have had a terrible night of it; he does his best – the poor old man! but it's all over with me."' It was in this room that Branwell died on Sunday 24 September 1848, aged 31, repenting that in all his life he had 'done nothing either great or good'.

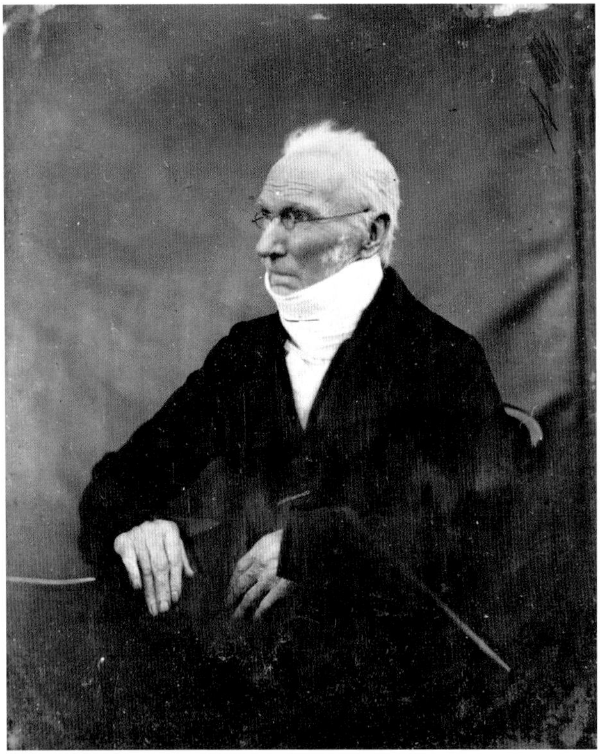

Mr Brontë photographed in old age.

In 1860 Elizabeth Gaskell, accompanied by her daughter Meta, paid her last visit to Mr Brontë, who was by this time confined to bed: 'we were taken into his bedroom; where everything was delicately clean and white, and there he was sitting propped up in bed in a clean nightgown, with a clean towel laid just for his hands to play upon…' Mr Brontë, having outlived his wife and children, died here on 7 June 1861, aged 84.

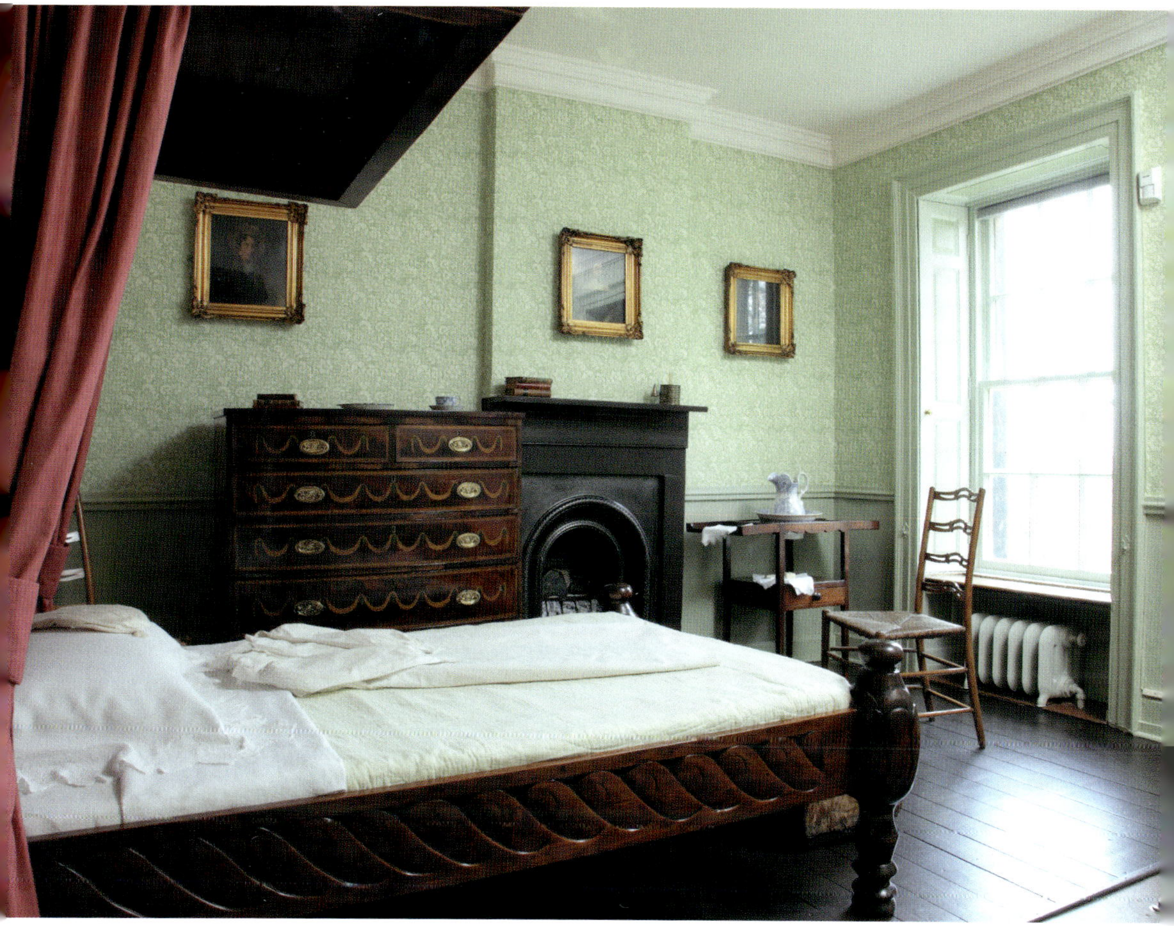

Mr Brontë's bedroom.

Analysis has revealed that this room was papered in the Brontë period, and that several shades of green were used on the woodwork - the panelling of the door was picked out in one shade, and the surrounding areas in another. These colours have been re-created and a matching wallpaper, reproduced from one of the period, has been used.

Branwell's Studio

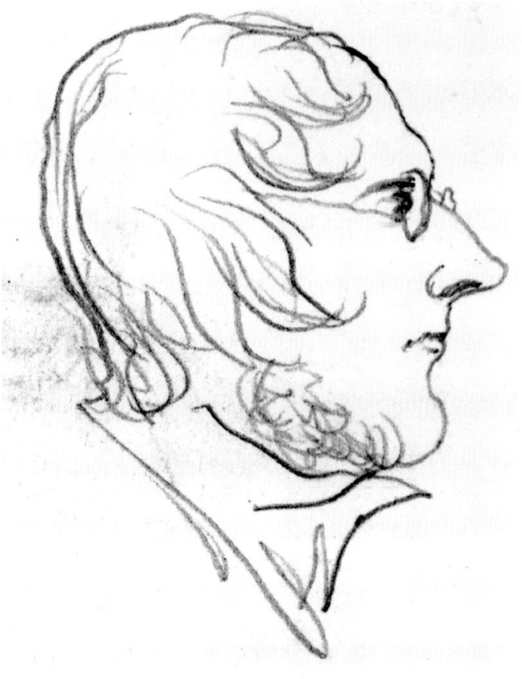

A caricature self-portrait by **Branwell Brontë**, *c.*1840.

THIS ROOM SERVED at one period as a studio for Branwell, who had trained with the Leeds artist William Robinson and hoped to become a professional portrait painter. Patrick Branwell Brontë occupied the privileged position of only boy in the family, with all expectations centred on him. His weakness of character and lack of application, however, meant that he failed in his chosen profession of artist, and eventually proved himself to be unemployable. In 1843 he became tutor to the son of Mr and Mrs Robinson at Thorp Green Hall, near York, where his sister Anne was employed as governess, but in July 1845 he was dismissed, apparently because of a love affair with Mrs Lydia Robinson. Branwell could not recover from this final blow, and turned increasingly to alcohol and opium. Inevitably his addiction ruined his health and contributed to his death from tuberculosis at the age of 31, in September 1848.

Following his funeral service, Branwell's life and death were summed up by his sister Charlotte: 'Branwell was his father's and his sisters' pride and hope in boyhood, but since manhood the case has been otherwise. It has been our lot to see him take a wrong bent…and now to behold the sudden early obscure close of what might have been a noble career.'

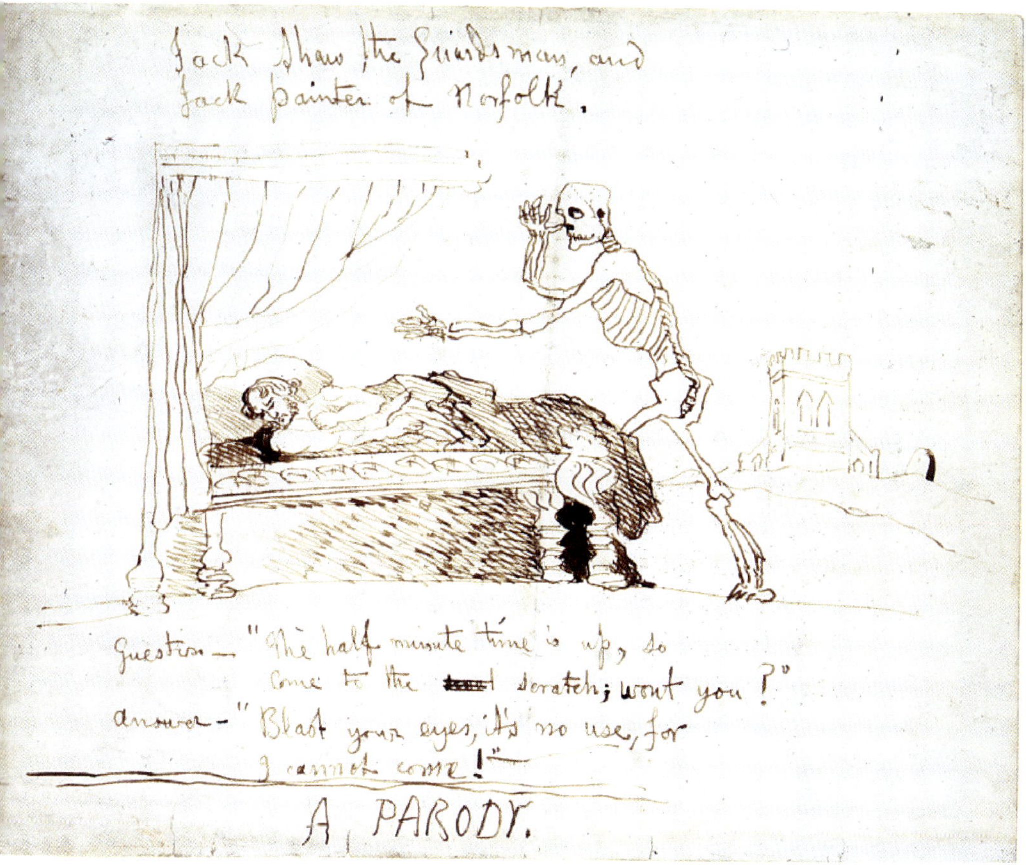

A Parody, Branwell's last surviving drawing, is a bleak and premonitory pen-and-ink sketch showing Death summoning him from sleep.

For much of the Brontë period, this room was in fact used as a bedroom; during Elizabeth Gaskell's visit to the Parsonage in 1853, Charlotte slept here. In the 1870s, when Wade extended the house, the window was blocked up and the room became a passageway to the new wing. Several years ago a scrap of wallpaper was found here, which has been dated to the Brontë period and is now reproduced on the walls.

TREASURES FROM THE COLLECTION

THE BRONTË PARSONAGE MUSEUM has the largest collection of Brontë material anywhere in the world. The collection contains a wide range of items, including manuscripts, letters, paintings and drawings, textiles, furniture, domestic artefacts and the family's personal possessions. The collection is a great scholarly resource, providing insights into the Brontës' lives and works. Today, the Brontë Society continues to add to its unrivalled collection of Brontëana.

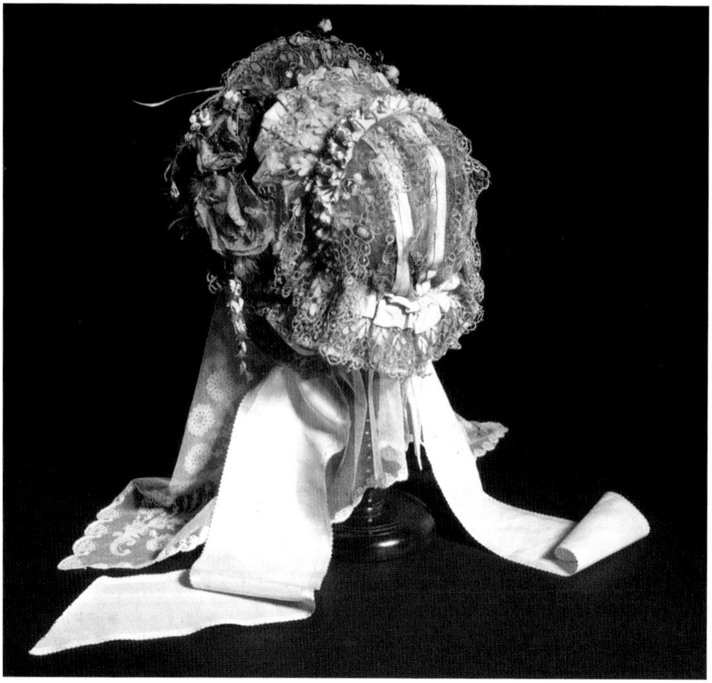

Charlotte's delicate **wedding bonnet** and veil are poignant reminders of the brief happiness which she shared with her husband, Arthur Bell Nicholls, until she died less than a year after their marriage. The bonnet has faded from its original white and green; on her wedding day, villagers described Charlotte as looking like 'a little snowdrop'.

RIGHT: Charlotte's copy of *The Atheist viewing the Dead Body of his Wife*, by A. B. Clayton.

BELOW: **Watercolour study** of a primrose by Charlotte Brontë. The strip of colours along the edge demonstrates her attempt at mixing colours.

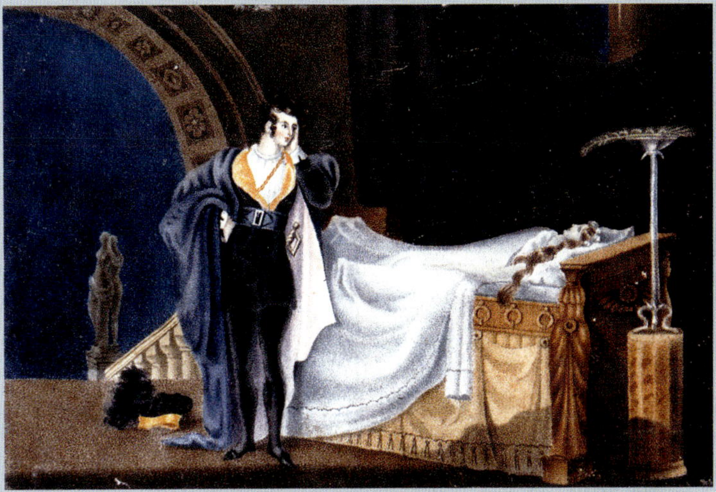

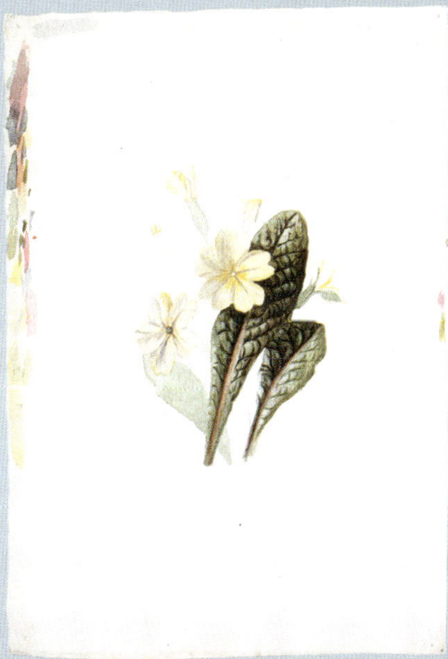

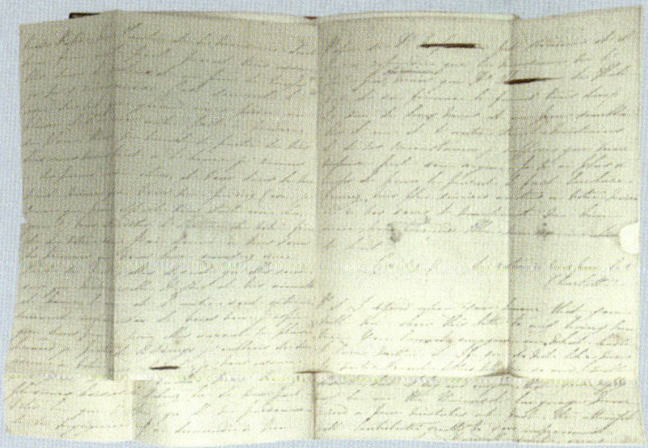

ABOVE: This **first edition** of Elizabeth Gaskell's *The Life of Charlotte Bronte* contains six original letters written by Charlotte Brontë to her close friend, Ellen Nussey. Together they chart the friendship between the two women, the first written in 1832, shortly after their schooldays ended, and the final letter shortly before Charlotte's death in 1855. The letters were purchased at Sotheby's in 2012 with generous support from the National Heritage Memorial Fund (NHMF) and donations from members of the Brontë Society.

RIGHT: This **pencil drawing** by Emily of the Brontës' dog, Grasper, was taken from life in January 1834. Of the few surviving paintings and drawings by Emily, the majority are studies of animals and birds, reflecting her love of the natural world.

BELOW: Emily's **mahogany artist's box** bears the trade label of R. Ackermann, of 96 Strand, and can be dated to after 1827, since that was when Ackermann moved into the premises. As well as remnants of paint and an ink bottle, the box contains an assortment of nibs, three miniature envelopes, sealing wax and a box of gummed labels.

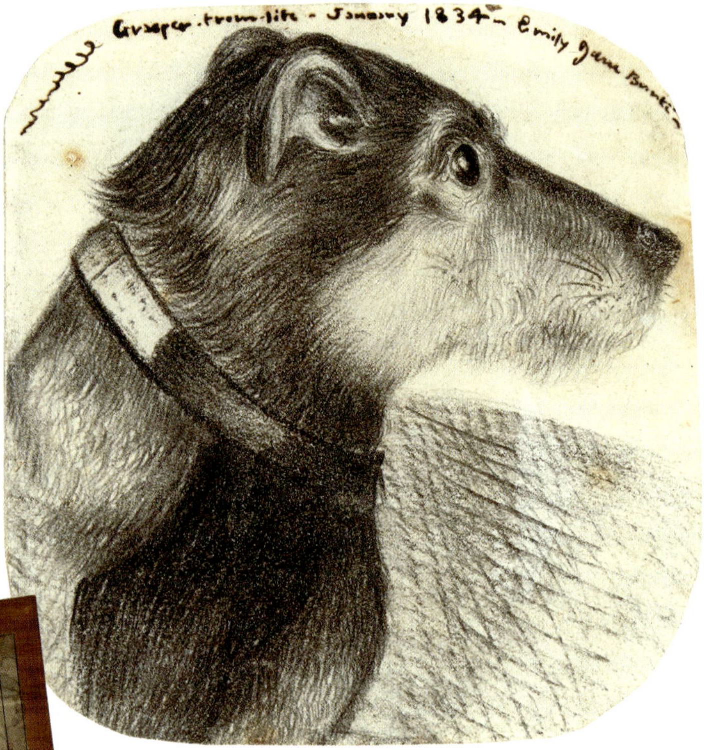

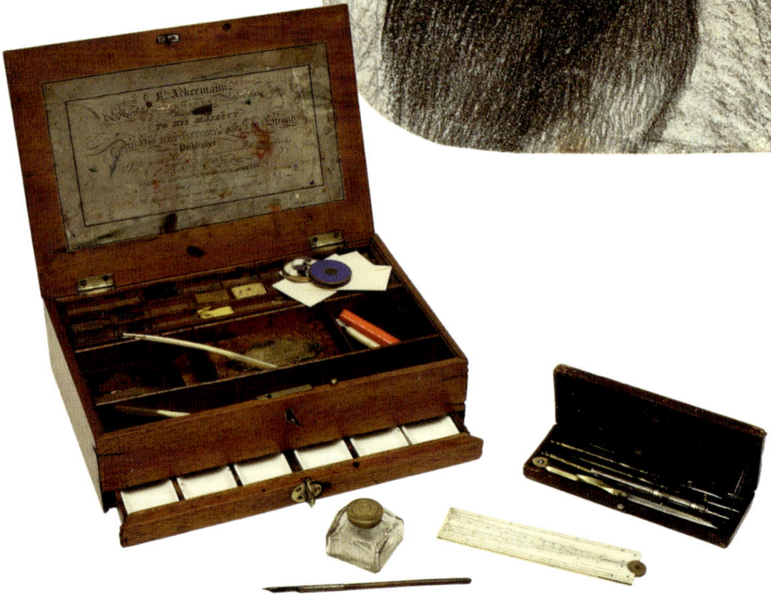

OPPOSITE: **A portrait of Anne** by her sister Charlotte, dated 17 April 1833. Three portraits of Anne by Charlotte survive, including two watercolours and this pencilled profile, in which Anne poses with a veil over her hair in the manner of a classical goddess.

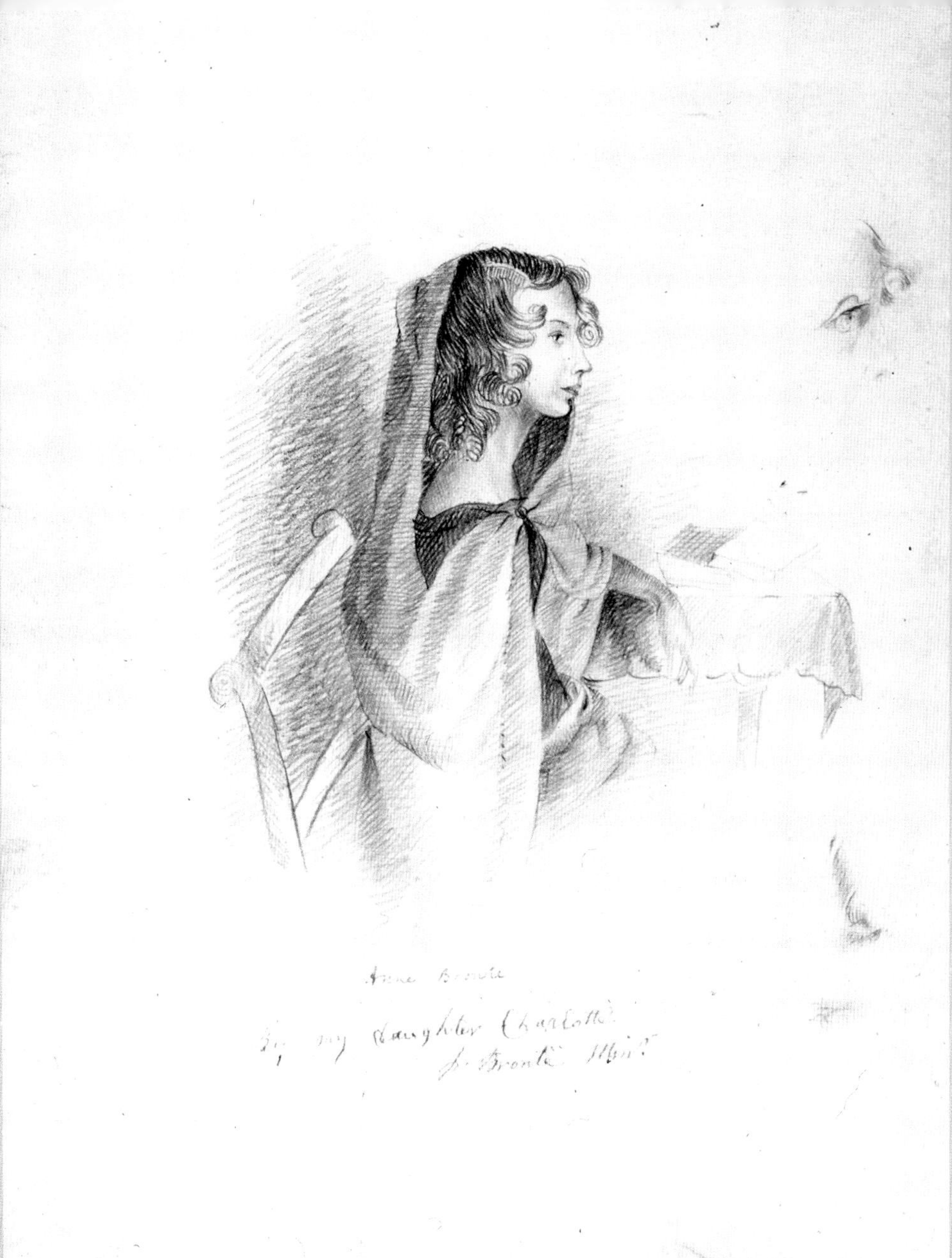
Anne Brontë
By my daughter Charlotte
P. Brontë Min.

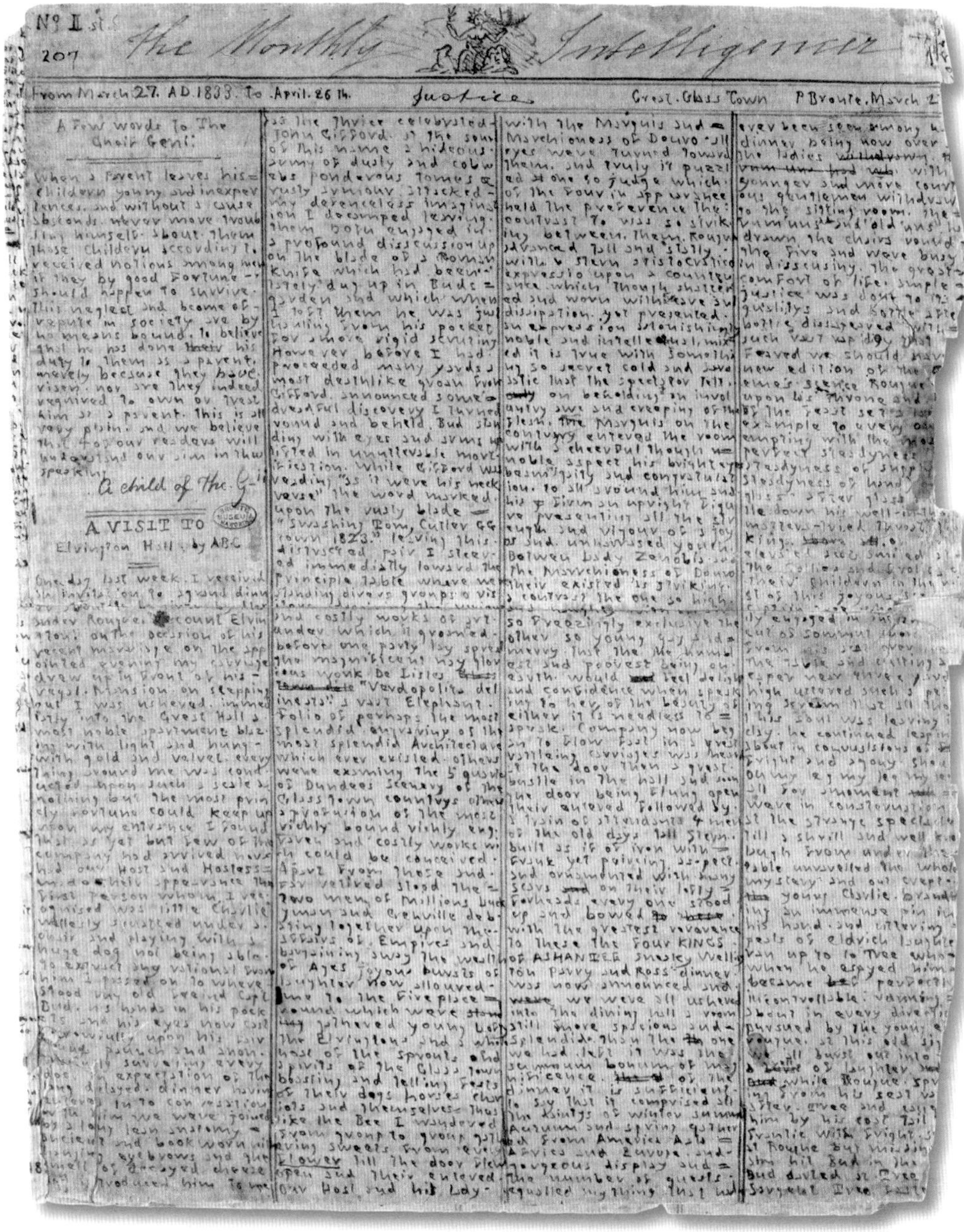
No II st.S
207
The Monthly Intelligencer

From March 27. AD 1833. To April. 26 th. Justice Great Glass Town P Bronte, March 2

A Few words to The Chief Geni:

When a Parent leaves his children young and inexperienced, and without a cause absconds never more troubling himself about them those children according to received notions among men if they by good Fortune should happen to survive this neglect and become of repute in society are by no means bound to believe that he has done his duty to them as a parent, merely because they have risen. nor are they indeed required to own or treat him as a parent. this is all very plain. and we believe that our readers will understand our aim in thus speaking.

A child of the G—

A VISIT TO
Elvington Hall, by ABC

One day last week I received an invitation to a grand dinner

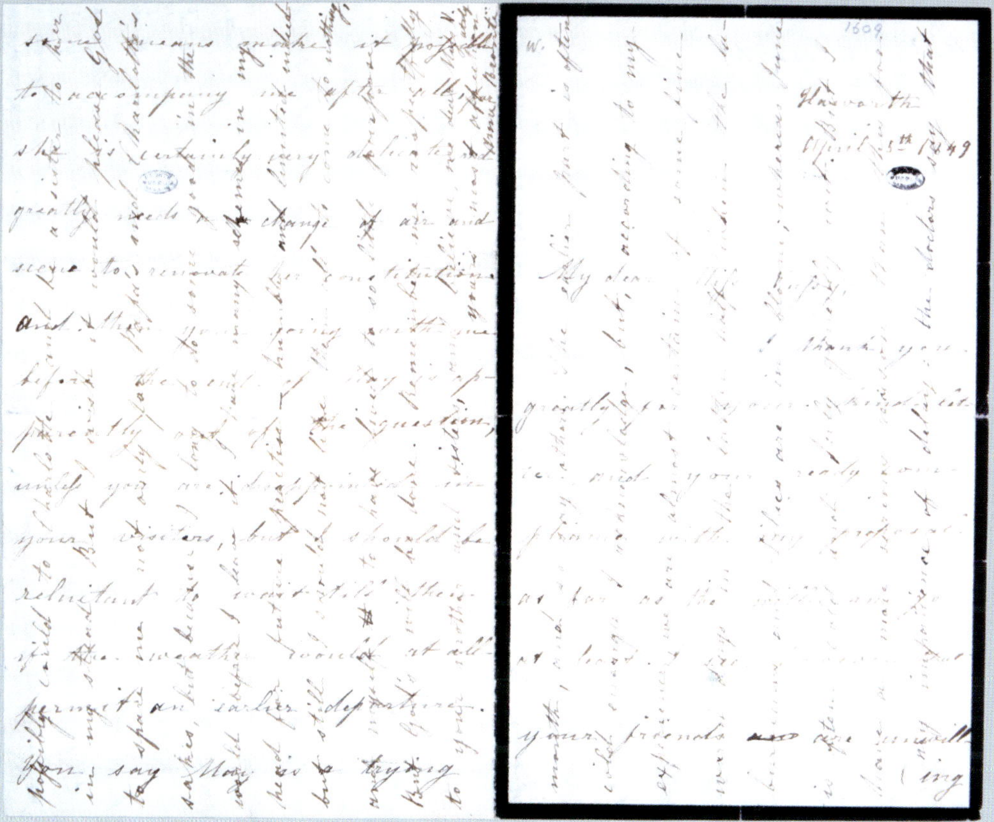

OPPOSITE: This **miniature newspaper**, *The Monthly Intelligencer*, was produced by Branwell between 27 March and 26 April 1833. The tiny handwriting makes many of the Brontës' manuscripts difficult to read without the aid of a magnifying glass.

ABOVE: Part of **Anne's last letter**, 5 April 1849, written to Ellen Nussey when Anne was seriously ill with tuberculosis, to ask if Ellen would travel with her and Charlotte to Scarborough, on the Yorkshire coast, in the hope that the sea air would help her. In the event, she died there. The letter is 'crossed', with lines written both horizontally and vertically, a common practice to save on postal costs.

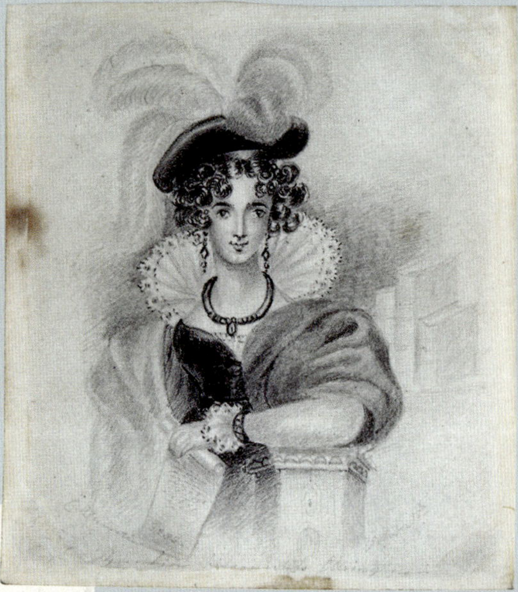

BELOW: **Branwell's portrait** of the Angrian character, Zamorna. In the Glasstown saga which the Brontës created as children, Zamorna was the eldest son of the Duke of Wellington, before he was made Duke of Zamorna and King of Angria.

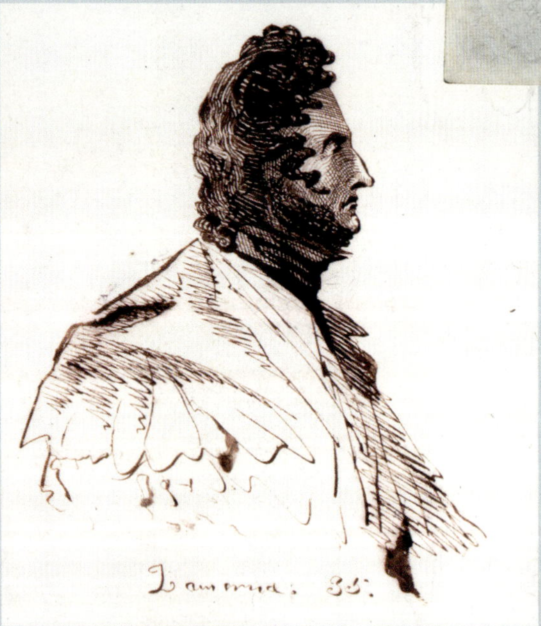

ABOVE: **Zenobia Ellrington**, the subject of this drawing by Charlotte, is a significant character in the Brontës' early writings, a strong intellectual woman and a forerunner of the great Brontë heroines to come. The drawing was purchased with the assistance of the V&A Purchase Grant Fund, The Art Fund and generous donations from members of the Brontë Society.

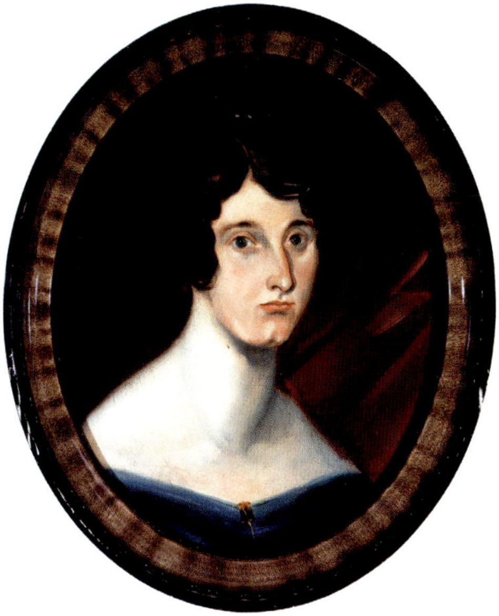

LEFT: Portrait by Branwell of **Maria Taylor**, *c.*1838-9. Maria was the daughter of Stephen and Mary Taylor of the Manor House at Stanbury; her father was one of the trustees of Haworth church and was instrumental in Patrick Brontë's being appointed to the living at Haworth. The portrait was purchased with the assistance of the V&A Purchase Grant Fund and The Art Fund.

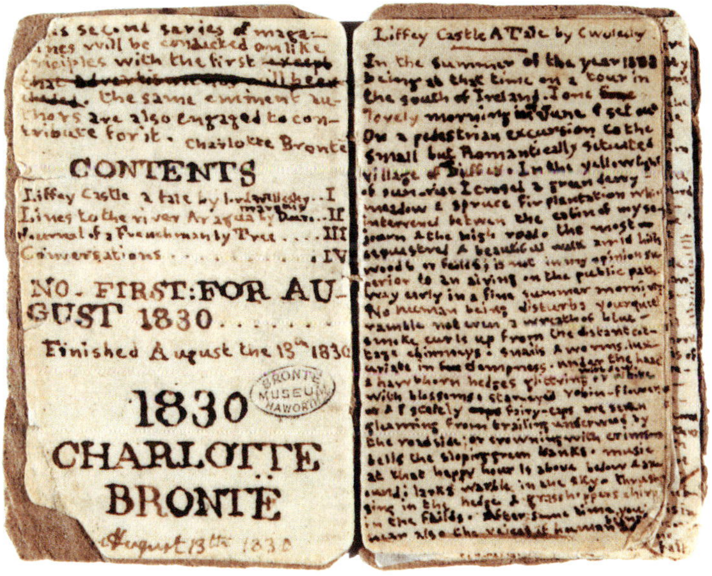

BELOW: In her early teens, Charlotte Brontë wrote six issues of *Blackwood's Young Mens Magazine*. These '**little books**' contain a mixture of prose and poetry written in a tiny script. Each issue includes a list of contents and carries advertisements and reviews, modelled on *Blackwood's Magazine*, which was an important influence on all the Brontë children. In the following year Charlotte began a 'second series', changing the title to the *Young Mens Magazine*, but assuring her readers that it was the work of 'the same eminent authors'. On Charlotte's death in 1855 her manuscripts passed to her widower, Arthur Bell Nicholls. In 1895 Nicholls was approached by the Brontë biographer, Clement Shorter, acting on behalf of the collector and forger T.J. Wise, who purchased the manuscripts, including the 'little books', and sold the bulk of them to a range of collectors. Four issues of the second series are now part of the Brontë Society's collection.

THE BRONTË SOCIETY

THE BRONTË SOCIETY, which administers the Brontë Parsonage Museum, was founded by a small group of enthusiasts in 1893. Many literary societies founded in this period did not survive, but the dedication of its early members held the Brontë Society together, and its reputation spread far beyond the West Riding of Yorkshire where it had originated. Today the Brontë Society is one of the most important literary societies in the world.

One of the Society's main objectives was to establish a museum to contain manuscripts, letters, drawings, paintings, and other personal

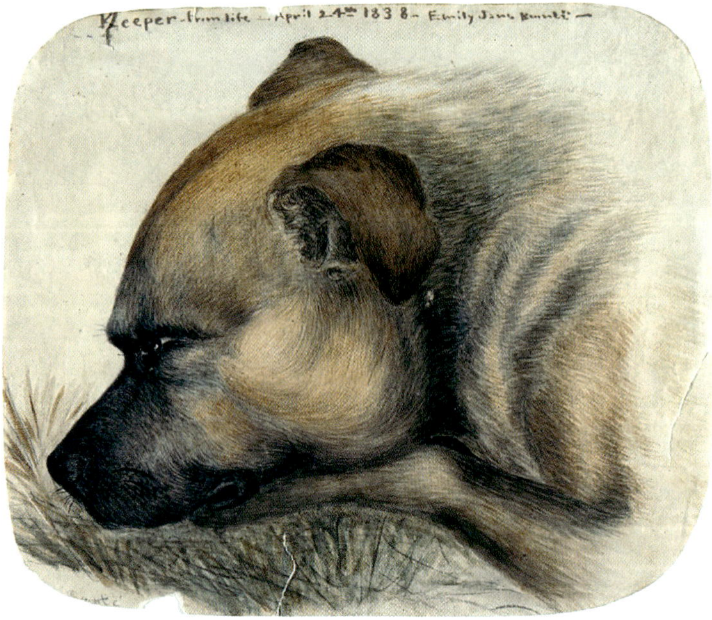

Emily's dog **Keeper**, drawn from life by Emily, is probably the best known of all the Brontë pets. The Brontës cared for a variety of animals at the Parsonage and Emily often made them the subjects of her drawings and paintings. Keeper was a bull mastiff with a ferocious reputation, who joined the mourners at Emily's funeral and spent many nights howling at the door of her empty bedroom.

relics of the Brontë family, editions of their works, writings on these works, and on the family, and photographs of places with which they were associated. A small museum was established in 1895, in a room above Haworth's Yorkshire Penny Bank (now the Visitor Information Centre), but from its foundation the Brontë Society hoped to acquire Haworth Parsonage. When, in 1927, the Parsonage was put up for sale for £3000, the Brontë Society's collection had outgrown the crowded one-room museum, but the Society's cash assets stood at less than £50. Local mill-owner Sir James Roberts, who described himself as 'one of the fast narrowing circle of Haworth veterans who remember the Parsonage family', not only bought the Parsonage, but part-funded its conversion, and a crowd of thousands arrived in Haworth to witness Sir James present the title deeds to the Society on 4 August 1928.

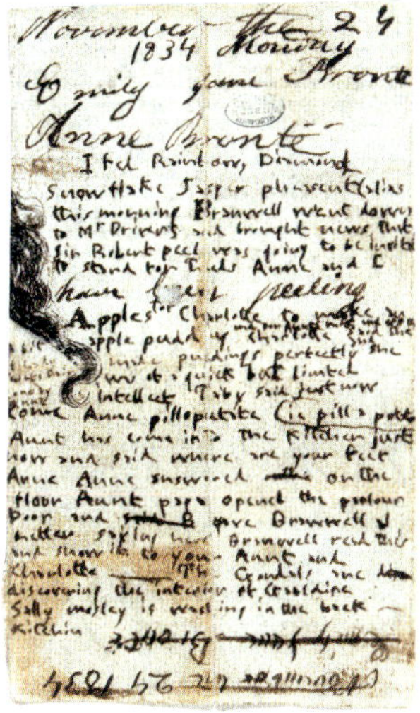
November the 24 1834 Monday
Emily Jane Bronte
Anne Bronte

A **diary paper**, dated 24 November 1834, jointly written by Emily and Anne.

Over the years the Brontë Society has sought to restore the Parsonage to its appearance in the Brontës' time. Although the household goods had been scattered far and wide after Patrick Brontë's death, many items were eventually returned. The Brontë Society is responsible for running the Brontë Parsonage Museum and caring for the collection, which continues to grow through gifts and acquisitions. The Society welcomes donations to fund our work, enabling us to add to the collection.

The Society aims to engage a wide range of people with the Brontës' works, illustrating their influence in world literature through our contemporary arts programme and award-winning education programme, promoting the imaginative teaching of their novels and poetry. The Society also campaigns to preserve the landscape and buildings the Brontë sisters would have known, and welcomes new members who wish to support our work.

If you are interested in becoming a member of The Brontë Society or making a donation, please contact the Society Administrator: telephone +44 (0) 1535 640195 or e-mail membership@bronte.org.uk

First published in 2013 by
Scala Arts & Heritage Publishers Ltd
21 Queen Anne's Gate
London SW1H 9BU
www.scalapublishers.com

ISBN 978-1-85759-879-7

Project manager: Jessica Hodge
Designer: Nigel Soper
Printed in Spain

10 9 8 7 6 5 4 3 2 1

British Library Cataloguing in Publication Data: a catalogue record for this book is available from the British Library.

Professor Ann Sumner is the Executive Director of the Brontë Society, and formerly the Director of the Birmingham Museums Trust.

Ann Dinsdale is Collections Manager at the Brontë Parsonage Museum.

Kathryn White is Development Manager at the Bagshaw Museum, formerly Curator at the Brontë Parsonage Museum.

For more information log on to our website www.bronte.org.uk, follow us on Facebook (Bronte Parsonage Museum) or on Twitter (@BronteParsonage).

FRONT COVER: The Brontë Parsonage Museum at Haworth, home of the Brontë family from 1820 to 1861.

FRONT FLAP: The moors near Haworth.

BACK COVER: Watercolour study of a merlin by Emily Brontë.

BACK FLAP: The dining room at Haworth.

INSIDE FRONT FLAP: One of six 'little books' written by Charlotte Brontë in her early teens.

INSIDE BACK FLAP: Early ambrotype photograph of Haworth Parsonage.

PAGE 1: Watercolour study of a wild rose by Charlotte Brontë.

PAGE 2: The Brontë Parsonage Museum.